Angels, Fools and Tyrants

Britons and Anglo-Saxons in Southern Scotland
AD *450–750*

Chris Lowe

Series editor: Gordon Barclay

CANONGATE BOOKS
with
HISTORIC SCOTLAND

THE MAKING OF SCOTLAND

Series editor:
Gordon Barclay

Other titles available:

WILD HARVESTERS:
The First People in Scotland

FARMERS, TEMPLES AND TOMBS:
Scotland in the Neolithic and Early Bronze Age

SETTLEMENT AND SACRIFICE:
The Later Prehistoric People of Scotland

A GATHERING OF EAGLES:
Scenes from Roman Scotland

SAINTS AND SEA-KINGS:
The First Kingdom of the Scots

THE SEA ROAD:
A Viking Voyage through Scotland

SURVIVING IN SYMBOLS:
A Visit to the Pictish Nation

First published in Great Britain in 1999
by Canongate Books Ltd, 14 High Street,
Edinburgh EH1 1TE

British Library Cataloguing-in-Publication Data
A catalogue record for this book is available on request
from the British Library

ISBN 0 86241 875 5

Series Design:
James Hutcheson, Canongate Books

Design:
Barrie Tullett

Printed in Spain by
Mateu Cromo, Madrid

Previous page
The site of the battle of Nechtansmere, near Forfar,
where Ecgfrith, king of Northumbria, was defeated
and killed on 20 May 685.
HISTORIC SCOTLAND

Contents

Dumbarton Rock (Alt Clut)
Alt Clut was the centre of the British kingdom in Strathclyde.
HISTORIC SCOTLAND

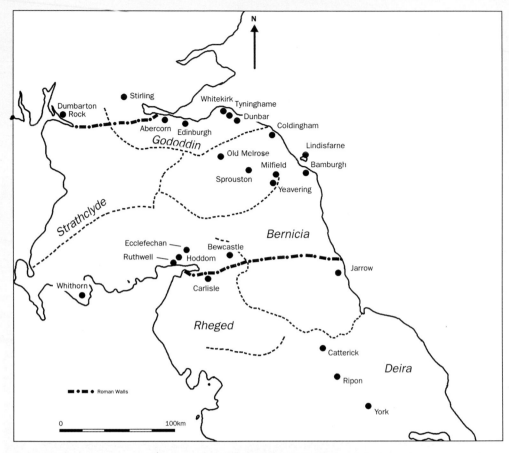

Location Map

Map showing the main places mentioned in the text.

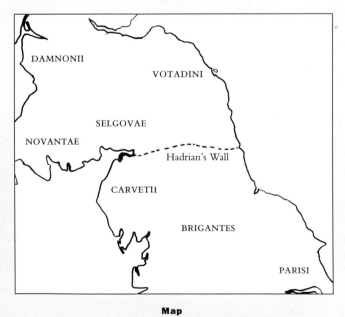

Map

Native tribes of southern Scotland and northern England,
compiled by Ptolemy of Alexandria in the second century.

Setting the Scene

This is the story of the Britons and Angles and their role in the creation of the country that we now know as Scotland. With the withdrawal of the Roman legions in the early fifth century, the local British tribes vied for supremacy. Increasingly throughout the sixth century, the English, the Angles of Northumbria, joined the struggle for control of the rich lands of southern Scotland, although no such country as 'Scotland' then existed. The words 'British' and 'English' now have different meanings. Throughout this book, 'British' refers to the native, indigenous population of the islands of present-day Britain. 'English' refers to the Angles, Saxons and Jutes who came to settle in their land. In southern Scotland we are principally concerned with the Angles of Deira and Bernicia, two British kingdoms which emerged in the period after the Romans' withdrawal and which were ultimately joined to form the Anglian kingdom of Northumbria, roughly equivalent to the area of modern-day Yorkshire, County Durham and Northumberland. Anglian and Anglo-Saxon are broadly interchangeable names for the northern English peoples of Northumbria and their culture.

Much of this book is about the states and petty kingdoms that grew up in northern Britain near the end of, and after, the Roman occupation. Inseparable from this process is the development of the Early Christian Church and the notion of *romanitas* – the searching out, preservation and upholding of things Roman – a theme which occurs again and again in the developing culture and attitudes of both Britons and Angles. We shall explore the relationships between the emerging British and Anglian kingdoms on the very fringes of what had been Roman Britain. The area of Scotland that concerns us is south of the Antonine Wall, down to and including Anglian Northumbria, north of Hadrian's Wall. The period we are interested in is between AD 450 and 750 – roughly the period in the history of southern Scotland between the withdrawal of the Roman garrisons and the passing of the first high water-mark of Anglian overlordship in the north. It is a time traditionally described as the 'Dark Ages' or more properly now as the Early Historic period.

The principal kingdoms which emerged in southern Scotland in the Early Historic period can be recognised in the old tribal groupings first recorded by the Roman geographer Ptolemy in the second century AD. On the east coast, centred on Lothian, were the Gododdin, Ptolemy's Votadini. In the west, centred on Alt Clut (Dumbarton Rock), was the early medieval kingdom of Strathclyde, the Damnonii of Ptolemy's *Geography*. To the south, along the shores of the Solway Firth and extending into modern-day Cumbria, was the ancient British kingdom of Rheged, a nebulous kingdom of uncertain extent and considered by some to have been a dubious, romantic fiction. Its Early Historic inhabitants would have been the descendants of the second-century Novantae and, in Cumbria, the Carvetii. Meanwhile, across the Pennines, there were the old British kingdoms of Deur, centred on the Vale of York, and Berneich to the north. Founded on the tribal areas of the Brigantes, these emerged during the course of the sixth century as the Anglian kingdoms of Deira and Bernicia to form Northumbria, the most powerful of the Anglo-Saxon kingdoms before the rise of Mercia in the eighth century and Wessex in the ninth century.

Petty Tyrants and Foolish Priests

*'Britain has kings, but they are tyrants…
Britain has priests but they are fools.'*

So wrote Gildas, a British priest, in his diatribe *De Excidio Britanniae* ('The Ruin of Britain'), written around the middle of the sixth century. The title 'Angels, fools and tyrants' draws together influential ideas about the relationship of the Britons and the Angles as presented by Gildas and taken up later by the historian Bede. Gildas' view was that, after the Roman withdrawal around AD 410, when the Britons were told to look to their own defence, there were the British 'tyrants' who were too lazy to resist the advances of the Scots and Picts from the north. They invited the Angles and Saxons into their country as mercenaries to protect them, in much the same way as the Romans had employed them earlier. However, they ended up fighting against them and against each other in a series of protracted civil wars. Then, there were also the British 'fools', the corrupt priests. Such condemnation by a Briton of his fellow priests suited Bede's purpose well for he had very real political reasons for presenting the British Church as having failed his heathen forefathers through their unwillingness, faithlessness and apparent lack of interest in converting the pagan Angles. Gregory, later pope, is said to have first encountered the Angles at a slave market in Rome. On asking after the race of some fair-faced, young,

heathen slaves, recently arrived at market from Britain, and on being told that they were called Angles (*Angli*), Gregory is reported to have said: 'Good, they have the face of angels (*angeli*), and such men should be fellow-heirs of the angels in heaven.' Gregory, as pope, was to be the moving force behind the Augustine mission of 597 to convert the English.

The works of giants

The Ruin

Splendid this rampart is, though fate destroyed it,
The city buildings fell apart, the works
Of giants crumble. Tumbled are the towers,
Ruined the roofs, and broken the barred gate,
Frost in the plaster, all the ceilings gape,
Torn and collapsed and eaten up by age.
Anon: *The Exeter Book*

The evocative Old English poem, 'The Ruin', is a reflective description of a Roman city, most probably Bath. There was no northern English poet to reflect upon the nature of the remains that would have been evident at places like Carlisle, Cramond, Inveresk or, of course, the Antonine and Hadrianic Walls themselves. It is easy, however, to picture the poet's 'public halls … with lofty gables', the noisy bath-houses and the 'many mead-halls filled with human pleasures'. Equally, we can picture the red curved roof shedding its tiles and the piles of rubble of which the poet speaks. These are familiar and detectable to archaeology. It is less easy, however, to people the city with its wealth of silver, gems and treasure, and the poet's host of gleaming, gold-adorned heroes, 'proud and flushed with wine'. The post-Roman inhabitants of 'The Ruin' come down to us as the 'mead-nurtured', 'mail-clad' and 'gold-torqued' warriors who are commemorated in the early British poem known as *Gododdin* and those

who feasted and drank in Hrothgar's mead-hall in the Anglo-Saxon heroic epic poem, *Beowulf*.

It matters little that 'The Ruin' was written after the period of this book and in another part of Britain, because the poem stands as a symbol for the decline and fall from past greatness. The significance of past Roman greatness, and the importance of linking oneself or one's institutions to that past, should not be underestimated. The architecture of the city is described as the 'works of giants' (*enta geweorc* in Old English), a phrase which appears elsewhere in Old English poetry to describe large ancient buildings, usually those of Roman origin. The poem also praises the 'resolute masons, skilled in rounded building' – an architecture founded on the use of stone, with lime for mortar and plaster, and glass for glazing. These were the highly desirable products of the age, the outward sign of the Roman 'good life'.

When these technologies reappeared in Northumbria in the latter part of the seventh century, in 674 in Benedict Biscop's monastic foundation at Wearmouth, it was as a result of bringing in masons and glaziers from Gaul. This was building in the Roman manner or *more Romanorum*. All of this was in marked contrast to what Bede described as *more Scottorum*: Finan's church on Lindisfarne, in the 650s, for example, was constructed not of stone but of hewn oak thatched with reeds in the manner of the Scots (i.e. Irish). Could the Northumbrians have got these Roman technologies from closer to home, among the Britons for example? Bede, perhaps reluctantly, admits that Ninian's church of Candida Casa, the 'White House' at Whithorn, was so-called because he built a church of stone; this, however, was regarded as 'unusual among the Britons'. Bede was writing a long time after the event and he may be recycling no more than a local tradition. How 'unusual' this really might have been depends largely on our view of how Romanised the native northern British kingdoms were in the fourth century or how 'sub-Romanised' they became during the course of the fifth and sixth centuries.

If Roman Britain ended not with a bang but a whimper, then that whimper is the period known to historians and archaeologists as the sub-Roman period. This period is generally understood to reflect a period of continuity in the fifth and sixth centuries, possibly into the seventh century too according to some scholars, when Roman practices, institutions and ways of doing things were taken over and developed by the various power-bases which were to emerge in the post-Roman world – a very different and much more dangerous world. With the collapse of the centralised authority with its widespread trading networks and means of control, power and influence passed to one of two emerging institutions. One – the one most closely integrated with the Roman past by virtue of its organisation, bureaucracy and learning – was the Church. The other was the powerful provincial potentate with his war-band, the Anglo–Saxon *comitatus* or the British *teulu*. Around these potentates, over time, the lordships, sub-kingdoms and kingdoms of sub-Roman Britain formed.

Northumbrian Expansion

The Northumbrian Angles who swept into southern Scotland in the early 600s were the fourth- or fifth-generation descendants of Germanic invaders from the region of Angulus, the area of modern-day Schleswig-Holstein in northern Germany. According to Bede, so many people migrated that the continental homeland was said to have remained unpopulated down to the time he was writing. However, these Northumbrians were not pure Teutons like Hengist and Horsa, for example, who grounded their keels on the beaches of Kent some time around the 470s. Nor did they form a monolithic Germanic nation which was pitted against an equally monolithic Brittonic nation, although this is often how the British and Anglian dynastic struggles of the Early Historic period are portrayed. Nevertheless the relationship between Angles and Britons in this period was typically one of continuing hostility, and no amount of special pleading for peaceful integration, continuity of institutions and estates, treaties and marriage alliances between Angles and Britons can ignore that fact: the historian, David Dumville, for example, has remarked 'It would be perverse to pretend that the result of such [Northumbrian] expansion was business as usual for the Britons, if under new management.'

In part, this is a reflection of the sources of evidence for what happened in the past. The problem of the historical and literary sources, whether Anglian or British, is that they are

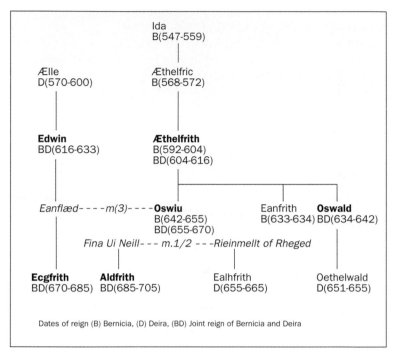

The Royal Houses of Deira and Bernicia
This diagram shows which kings reigned over Deira and Bernicia in the sixth and seventh centuries, and their periods of reign.

naturally biased to one or other point of view. The sources also derive overwhelmingly from within an ecclesiastical or monastic setting. After all, Bede's *Ecclesiastical History of the English People* was not a history of England, far less one of its non-English peoples. On the whole, British sources, likewise, take a similar but opposed line, presenting the *cymry* (fellow-countrymen) of western Britain, that is to say Strathclyde, Cumbria, Wales and Cornwall (and even Brittany in some contexts), as a single nation opposed to the aggressions of the Saxons. The call to arms of this greater British nation to expel the Saxon invaders is a motif which was to permeate British writing for centuries to come. 'Armes Prydein', a tenth-century Welsh poem which called for a mixed alliance of Britons, Scots and the Vikings of Dublin to rid the island of the Saxons, could be

would provide the Northumbrian kings, or any British princeling who had the mind to, with the riches to reward their followers and to enhance their own power and that of their lineage. Access to the western seaboard, whether through Cumbria or along the Solway, would also provide an opportunity to control the trading networks of the Irish Sea basin.

Northumbrian expansion into southern Scotland, with the important exception of Edwin who was from Deira, is essentially the story of the rise to dominance of the Bernician line under Æthelfrith, his sons (Oswald and Oswiu) and grandsons (Ecgfrith and Aldfrith). It begins, however, two generations earlier with

considered a direct descendant of the much earlier (and much less territorially ambitious) British text known as *Gododdin*. The subject of the 'noble British resistance' is also the very stuff of the legend of King Arthur.

In the seventh century, taking over southern Scotland would have presented a tempting prospect for the Angles. The fertile farmlands of Lothian and Fife, and the rich pasture and mineral-rich areas of Dumfries and Galloway,

Bede's brief statement '547: Ida began to reign, from whom the Northumbrian royal family trace their origin'. Further information on Ida and his immediate descendants derives only from the *Historia Brittonum* which tells us that Ida established his stronghold at Din Guoaroy (Bamburgh).

The *Historia Brittonum* is an early ninth-century compilation of earlier documents, put together by a Welsh monk called Nennius who tells us in his preface that he has 'made a heap' of all the documents and traditions that he could find. This 'ragbag' nonetheless includes fragments of what are regarded as genuine elements of a lost 'Northern British History', probably composed in the northern British kingdom of Strathclyde. The loss of much of this northern literary and historical tradition is probably one of the greatest cultural tragedies that befell north Britain in the Early Historic period.

The peak of Northumbrian domination of the north came to an end with Ecgfrith's defeat by the Picts at the battle of Nechtansmere in 685. The battle scene on the reverse side of the Pictish symbol stone at Aberlemno churchyard possibly commemorates this defeat of the Northumbrian Angles. Known to British historical tradition as the battle of Llyn Garan, the 'Pool of the Crane', the battle site has been identified with Dunnichen Moss near Forfar. Ecgfrith's defeat was clearly considered by Bede to represent a turning point in the northern affairs of the Northumbrian kings. After this, according to Bede, 'the hopes and strengths of the English kingdom began to ebb and fall away. For the Picts recovered their own land which the English had formerly held, while the Irish who lived in Britain and some part of the British nation (*pars Brettonum*) recovered their independence, which they have now enjoyed for about forty-six years.' The *pars Brettonum* is generally taken to refer to the Britons of Strathclyde. Northumbrian interest in northern British and Pictish politics, however, certainly continued. There are records of northern campaigns by later Northumbrian kings and their lieutenants, principally against the Picts, down to the middle of the eighth century. Around 750, the Northumbrian king Eadberht annexed the district of Kyle from the kingdom of

Strathclyde. In all, 'Scotland between the Walls' was to remain part of the Anglian kingdom of Northumbria for some three hundred years until it was ceded to the Scots in 973. Scottish conquest was finally confirmed by the Battle of Carham in 1018.

Gododdin and the battle of Catraeth

Many battles between the Angles and Britons are recorded in the sources. Some involved coalitions of the British kingdoms; others involved Anglo-British alliances against other Anglian or British kingdoms. In some, pagans and Christians would ally against other Christian kingdoms. One of the most famous is the battle of Catraeth, identified as Catterick or more particularly the Roman fortified town at Catterick Bridge, known as Cataractonium or Cataracta, situated to the north of the Vale of York in Deira. The battle was traditionally dated to around 600, but modern scholarship has now tended to favour an earlier date, around 540 or 570.

The early British poem, *Gododdin*, is a collection of heroic death-songs which eulogise the 300 or so warriors or chieftains from the British kingdom of Gododdin who set out from Din Eidyn, the hillfort of Eidyn (identified as Edinburgh), to do battle against the English at Catraeth.

In the orthodox interpretation, the warriors were feasted for a year in the hall of Mynyddog Mwynvawr, Mynyddog the Wealthy, ostensibly the chieftain of Din Eidyn. Below the burning tapers and in the light of the blazing log fires, they drank their mead and wine in cups of glass, silver and gold, reclining on feather-cushioned couches, while the plans for the campaign were made.

The army of the Gododdin was a grand

Castle Rock, Edinburgh
Aerial view of the Castle Rock,
Edinburgh: a British stronghold, perhaps
the Din Eidyn of the poem *Gododdin*.
HISTORIC SCOTLAND

the sea of Iudeu' (the Firth of Forth).

Setting out from Din Eidyn, the army of the Gododdin coalition rode off to be wiped out at Catterick. Din Eidyn is usually identified with the Castle Rock in Edinburgh, where recent finds indicate occupation in the Late Roman period. The case for the fort being on Arthur's Seat (the 'mountain' in the heart of Edinburgh), however, is equally strong. The recent discovery of a hoard of Bronze Age axes testifies to the site's ritual significance at an earlier date: possibly it remained a central place of some importance to the Votadini/Gododdin of later times. In any event, the expedition to Catterick appears to have been a complete disaster: only one, or three, of the chieftains returned, depending on which of the various texts of the poem is correct.

alliance of the kind much vaunted in British tradition. It was a sizable force: some estimates have put it as large as 24,000 or more, allowing a contingent of 80 for each warrior, along the lines of a Roman military expedition. In addition to the men of Gododdin itself, it included warriors from Strathclyde, Ayrshire, the British kingdom of Elmet in Yorkshire, Gwynedd in North Wales, as well as heathen Picts from 'beyond Bannog' (the Fintry, Kilsyth, Campsie and Kilpatrick Hills) and from 'beyond

Much ink has been spilled over when the poem *Gododdin* was composed, how it was later transmitted in written form, the period and events that it describes, the size of the armies, their tactics and, indeed, even the ethnic make-up of the two sides in the conflict. But the story seems very simple: a small, highly mobile and mounted force of gallant Britons striking hard against the heart of the pagan Anglian kingdoms, far to the south and many miles from home.

The Battle of Catraeth

The battle of Catraeth, like other battles in this period, was a savage and bloody affair. Men were hewn down like rushes, blades were reddened, spears splattered and ravens feasted on the bodies of the dead and dying as they lay on the battlefield. The reconstruction painting shows Yrfai mab Wolstan's attack on the massed ranks of the Northumbrian Angles and their ?British allies. Yrfai wears a Roman helmet, presented to him by Gwlyget lord of Gododdin as a mark of his rank as Lord of Eidyn. Perhaps it had been plundered many years before from a consignment of military equipment which had been left abandoned at Cramond Roman Fort. Perhaps helmets such as these had acquired symbols of status with the passing of time. Other aspects of his dress and equipment similarly reflect the conservative tastes and pseudo-Roman trappings of the Gododdin royal household.

CHRIS BROWN

It was usual for him to be mounted upon a high-spirited horse defending Gododdin, at the forefront of the men eager for fighting. It was usual for him to be fleet like a deer. It was usual for him to attack Deira's retinue. It was usual for Wolstan's son — though his father was no sovereign lord — that what he said was heeded. It was usual for the sake of the mountain court that shields be broken through and reddened before Yrfai Lord of Eidyn.

(*Gododdin* B².28)

Not everything is necessarily as clear as it seems. Mynyddog mwynvawr, for example, is traditionally identified as the otherwise unknown chieftain of Din Eidyn. An alternative interpretation, however, is that the words *mynyddog mwynvawr*, meaning respectively 'mountainous' and 'wealthy' or 'luxurious', refer not to a person but to a place, 'the luxurious mountain court' (perhaps Din Eidyn itself), or act as a metaphor for the British kingdoms of the north. Such an interpretation does not, however, leave the Gododdin leaderless. Two human candidates emerge. One is Gwlyget of Gododdin, who was the only one of the presumably many locally based warriors who was given the epithet of the tribe and kingdom: 'of Gododdin'. Previously understood to have been 'Mynyddog's' steward, Gwlyget emerges as the likely hereditary lord of Gododdin, the provider of the feast for 'the mountain court' and the sponsor of the fateful campaign. The second figure is Yrfai son of Golistan, described as 'Lord of Eidyn', who has been put forward as the likely leader of the Gododdin force at Catraeth. Significantly, the name Golistan has been recognised as an Old Welsh rendering of Anglo-Saxon Wolstan or Wulfstan; as a result it has been suggested that there may have been a small Anglian military elite operating within the upper levels of the royal court of Gododdin.

The recognition that the warriors of Gododdin were led into battle by an Anglo-British half-caste, described in the eulogy as 'Lord of Eidyn', certainly turns on its head many of the previously accepted ideas of Anglo-British relations in this period. The Angles at Catterick, conversely, may have been under *British* leadership. In the *Book of Taliesin*, in a text known as *Gweith Gwen Ystrat* ('The Battle of the White Valley'), Urien of Rheged, one of the most renowned of the northern British kings, is described as the Lord of Catraeth, 'the battle-victorious, cattle-rich sovereign'. Some commentators have suggested that the disaster of Catraeth, as described in *Gododdin*, and Urien's victory at Gwen Ystrat represent the same battle viewed from opposite sides. Rather than being a glorious all-British crusade against the Angles, the battle of Catraeth may be better considered solely in terms of the domestic politics of southern Scotland – an essentially British struggle between the competing houses of Rheged and Gododdin, in some form of alliance with, respectively, the Anglian kingdoms of Deira and Bernicia.

The pagan Bernician king Æthelfrith, accorded the epithet *Flesaurs* ('the Artful') in British sources, emerges as the first of the Anglian Northumbrian kings whom we know to have been active in southern Scotland. According to Bede,

> he ravaged the Britons more extensively than any other English ruler… For no ruler or king had subjected more land to the English race or settled it, having first either exterminated or conquered the natives.

In 603 Æthelfrith defeated Aedán mac Gabráin, king of the Dál Riata, at the battle of Degsastan. It was a costly battle, both for Aedán, who lost almost his entire army, and for Æthelfrith, whose brother Theodbald was killed, together with all his following. Degsastan is traditionally identified with Dawston in Liddesdale, but the case for Addinston, possibly a corruption of *aet Aegdanes stan* ('Aedan's stone'), near Lauder in Berwickshire, has also been made. Whether it was fought at Dawston, Addinston or elsewhere in what historians have called 'the northern battle zone', this victory was clearly considered by Bede to have been a turning point: 'From that time no Irish king in Britain has dared to make war on the English race to this day.'

Strongholds and Centres of Power

One of the principal strongholds of the Britons of southern Scotland, the *civitas Brettonum munitissima*, was Alt Clut, Dumbarton Rock, the centre of the British kingdom of Strathclyde. A naturally defensible site, located at the confluence of the Clyde and the Leven rivers and with access to the trading networks of the Irish Sea, the site was of strategic importance throughout the Early Historic period. Among its early rulers may have been Coroticus, to whom St Patrick, Apostle of Ireland, had addressed an open letter, and Rhydderch who fought alongside Urien at the siege of Lindisfarne in 590. In Adomnán's *Life of St Columba*, he is referred to as 'Rodercus son of Tothal, ruler at the Rock of the Clyde'.

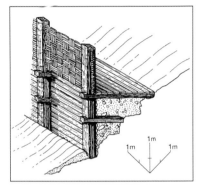

Reconstruction of the Rampart at Alt Clut
LESLIE ALCOCK

Alt Clut, a British Stronghold
Looking north towards Alt Clut (Dumbarton Rock), with the Kilpatrick Hills (part of the range known as 'Bannog') in the distance.
HISTORIC SCOTLAND

Trial excavations at Alt Clut in the 1970s revealed the remains of an earth, rubble and timber rampart, located at the lower edge of a steep slope on the eastern side of the rock. Probably constructed of large, squared oak beams up to 30cm across, and forming a rampart about 2m wide and at least 2m high, probably with a breastwork on top, it would have formed a formidable defence. Radiocarbon dating of the burnt timbers suggests that the rampart could have been constructed as early as the late sixth century.

Finds from the site included a small collection of Romano-British material, principally fine tableware of first- to fourth-century date and possibly a 'reliquary' import to the site in the Early Historic period. Fragments of amphorae (known as B-ware), in which wine had been imported from the Mediterranean in the late fifth or sixth centuries, and sherds of E-ware, a high-quality table-ware imported from Gaul from the late sixth to the early eighth centuries, indicate the high status of the site's occupants and their access to the continental 'luxury goods' market. This is reinforced by the discovery of fragments of glass vessels, possibly beakers, cups and bowls, of a similar date and source as the imported table-ware. Previously dismissed as fragments of glass which were collected for reworking into beads, bangles and inlays, the finds from Alt Clut are now considered to represent the remains of actual vessels. Like the warriors of *Gododdin* and the post-Roman inhabitants of *The Ruin*, the Early Historic rulers on the Rock of Clyde could have supped wine from 'brimming glass vessels'. The presence of small thin-walled crucibles also testifies to fine jewellery-making on the site. The nature of the archaeological evidence, in combination with the early historical references to the site, clearly mark it out as the centre of a royal household. Fine metalworking is also evident from excavations at Mote of Mark, a British and later an Anglian stronghold on the Solway coast in Kirkcudbrightshire.

Other princely centres are also known. Din Eidyn, the principal seat of the Gododdin, is one. A place known to British tradition as Iudeu and to Bede as *urbs Guidi* is probably another. Although sometimes identified with the Roman forts at Cramond or Inveresk,

Grubenhäuser

Grubenhaus, meaning 'pit-' or 'sunken-building', is a term taken from German archaeology to describe a type of structure which appears as a small, rectangular pit with post- or stake-holes along its sides and larger post-holes at its gable ends. They are typically up to 6 x 4m and 0.5m deep. Common in their continental homeland at this period, their appearance in the British Isles has been taken as a reliable indicator of Anglo-Saxon settlement.

The *Grubenhaus* was the first, and for a long time the only, type of building known on Anglo-Saxon rural sites. The effects of plough-truncation mean that a sunken-featured building, cut into the subsoil, will survive longer than the post-holes or floors associated with any timber-built surface structure.

The first recognised example of a *Grubenhaus*, described as flimsy and suggesting a squalid existence for its inhabitants, was discovered in Oxfordshire in 1857. The first Anglo-Saxon settlement to be excavated, at Sutton Courtenay in Berkshire in the 1920s (and only the *Grubenhäuser* were recognised), was said by its excavator to reflect the particularly primitive culture of its inhabitants. As late as 1948, a survey of ancient monuments compiled by the Council for British Archaeology could assert that the Anglo-Saxons were culturally primitive, their buildings wretchedly flimsy and their architecture incompetent. All of this was markedly at variance with what was known of their skill in fine metalworking and jewel-smithing, the sumptuousness of the timber hall described in *Beowulf* or the craftsmanship in timber that would have gone into making the Sutton Hoo ship in Suffolk, discovered just before the outbreak of war in 1939. It also ran counter to the types of aisled and other substantial surface-buildings that continental archaeology had been finding since the 1920s.

Before the late 1950s, Anglo-Saxon archaeology was principally represented by the artefacts and structures from its pagan cemeteries and a handful of 'rude huts'. Aerial photography and improved excavation techniques were to provide the grand halls and other buildings which had been so long anticipated. Brian Hope-Taylor and his excavations at Yeavering in Northumberland led the way in the late 1950s.

Iudeu is more generally thought to have been the Castle Rock at Stirling, possibly the centre of the ancient British kingdom or province of Manaw Gododdin. The district, around the head of the Firth of Forth (the sea of Iudeu in *Gododdin*), is preserved today in the place-names Sla**mannan** and Clack**mannan**. According to British sources, it was at Iudeu in 654 that the Northumbrian king Oswiu was forced to hand over to Penda, the pagan king of Mercia, and his British allies all the riches of the city, an event known as the 'Distribution of Iudeu'. No archaeological remains of this period have yet been found at either site, however.

Other, perhaps lesser, British strongholds are also known in southern Scotland and Northumbria. Many, such as Edinburgh, and possibly Stirling also (if correctly identified as the site of Oswiu's refuge), were taken over as Anglian strongholds and centres of power.

Bamburgh, the site of Ida's stronghold in the sixth century and described as the royal city of the Northumbrian kings in the seventh century, is known in British sources as Din Guoaroy. The place-name contains the element '*din*' for fort indicating that it was the site of an earlier British fortification. It was renamed Bebbanburh by Æthelfrith after his wife, Bebba. There is a late account in one of the versions of the *Anglo-Saxon Chronicle* that Ida first enclosed the natural citadel of Bamburgh Rock with a palisade and later a rampart. There is, however, a great deal of uncertainty about how events attributed to this early period came to be incorporated into the later *Chronicle*. Unlike Alt Clut, no traces of the early defences have yet been found at Bamburgh but archaeological excavations, focused around a small knoll which forms the seaward end of the citadel, have revealed a succession of deposits and artefacts indicative of activity spanning the pre-Roman Iron Age to

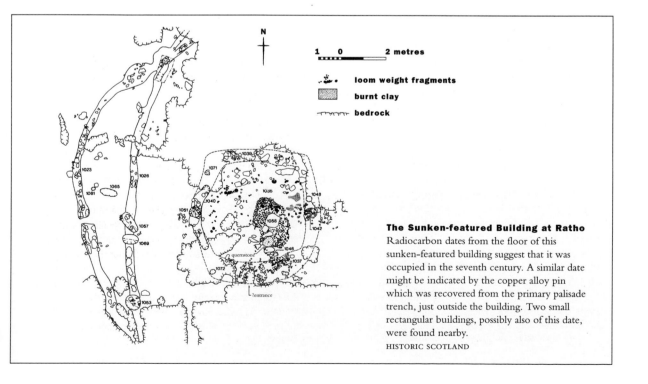

1   0   2 metres

loom weight fragments

burnt clay

bedrock

The Sunken-featured Building at Ratho
Radiocarbon dates from the floor of this sunken-featured building suggest that it was occupied in the seventh century. A similar date might be indicated by the copper alloy pin which was recovered from the primary palisade trench, just outside the building. Two small rectangular buildings, possibly also of this date, were found nearby.
HISTORIC SCOTLAND

Grubenhäuser are now interpreted as ancillary buildings, stores or workshops. Weaving appears to have been one of the principal activities associated with these buildings: clay loom-weights, spindle-whorls and other items associated with textile production are frequently found in them. Sunken below ground level and therefore damp, it has been said that such an atmosphere makes weaving easier, particularly the working of flax into linen.

In recent years, *Grubenhäuser* have been found further and further north. Examples are now known from Scotland. The crop-mark evidence from Sprouston, near Kelso, has revealed the outlines of a remarkable Anglian township, complete with timber halls, cemetery and sunken-featured buildings. Recent investigations at Dunbar (East Lothian) and near Ratho (West Lothian) have both produced sunken-featured buildings with the expected loom-weights for weaving, left in line where they fell when the buildings burnt down. Other excavated examples of the building-type are known from the Northumbrian monastery at Hoddom (Dumfriesshire): one was used as a corn-drying kiln, another as a smithy.

Aerial photography has now shown that the building-type extends over a wide area of the eastern seaboard from Fife to Moray. Indeed, rectangular and annexed timber halls, possibly of Yeavering-type, are also known from this area. None, however, has yet been excavated and their date and cultural associations are unknown.

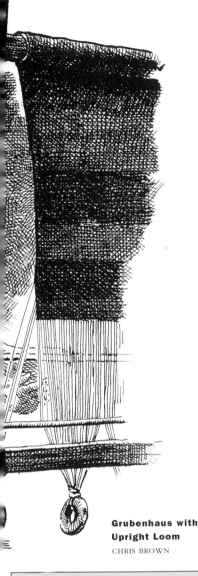

the seventh century AD. Massive dumps of charcoal and fire-reddened clay on the knoll have been interpreted as the remains of an early signal beacon.

Some four miles up the coast from Bamburgh is Lindisfarne, an ideal safe haven to rest or assemble a fleet, Bernician or otherwise. Known in British sources as Metcaud, it is the place where, in or around 590, Urien of Rheged, together with Rhydderch Hen, ruler of the Strathclyde Britons, and two other British kings, besieged one of Ida's sons for three days and three nights. It was also where Urien was treacherously assassinated by one of his own side. The Rock of Beblowe, also named after Bebba and, like Bamburgh, the site of a later castle, is the most naturally defensible site on the island and the likely focus of an early stronghold. Some have identified it with an otherwise unlocated *urbs Broninis*, another seventh-century Anglian royal centre with a British name.

Another example of the Anglian takeover of an earlier British stronghold comes from Dunbar (East Lothian). The place-name Dynbaer, meaning 'summit fort', was first recorded in an early eighth-century account concerning the imprisonment there, in about 680, of Bishop Wilfrid, one of the most powerful ecclesiastical rulers of the time. The place is described as a royal town or stronghold. In the late 1980s, excavations on the headland (opposite the later castle) revealed a complex series of buildings and deposits which span the pre-Roman Iron Age down to modern times.

Occupied as an enclosed promontory fort during the Roman period and controlling access to the natural harbour of

Grubenhaus with Upright Loom
CHRIS BROWN

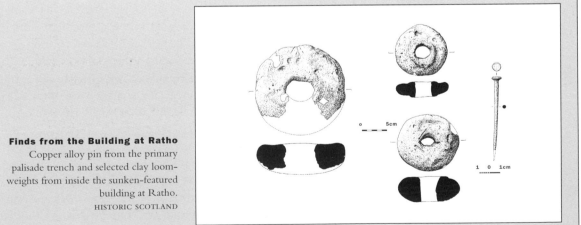

Finds from the Building at Ratho
Copper alloy pin from the primary palisade trench and selected clay loom-weights from inside the sunken-featured building at Ratho.
HISTORIC SCOTLAND

Fragment of a Gold and Garnet Object
This fragment is possibly one end of a cross-pendant. Only 1cm long, it is similar to one which was found in St Cuthbert's tomb in Durham Cathedral in 1827. Early seventh century in date, it possibly came north with Bishop Wilfrid, via the fine gold and garnet jewellery workshops of Kent.
SCOTTISH URBAN ARCHAEOLOGICAL TRUST

Lamerhaven immediately to the east, the site at Dunbar is thought to have functioned as a trading port for the major Votadinian hillfort at Traprain Law. However, the lack of imported artefacts from the site is in marked contrast to the collection from Alt Clut and emphasises the very real differences that existed between the east- and the west-coast trading routes.

The primary Northumbrian occupation of the Dunbar site is marked by a number of timber buildings, set around a series of cobbled open spaces or courtyards. Nearby was a sunken-featured building or *Grubenhaus*, used for weaving.

The buildings of the primary settlement at Dunbar were subsequently replaced by a series of timber structures with stone-footings. This is a change which has been seen at other Anglian sites in the north – the monastic sites at Whitby, Hartlepool, Whithorn and Hoddom. Where dated, it appears to be a feature of the eighth century.

To the north of the refurbished settlement, but mostly outwith the area excavated, one of the most remarkable of the structures found at Dunbar was erected: a mortared stone building, interpreted as a royal hall. Possibly it replaced an earlier timber hall on roughly the same site. Near here, a small gold and garnet object was found from one of the courtyards; it may have been part of a cross-pendant that would have been worn around the neck of a high-ranking churchman, possibly Wilfrid himself.

A mortar-mixer was also found. Mortar-mixers are rare features in Anglo-Saxon archaeology and the Dunbar example is a unique find in Scotland in this period. Plaster, mortar or concrete would be formed by mixing lime together with an aggregate, usually sand or gravel, and water. Limestone, burnt to produce quicklime, is locally available at Dunbar but shells were also used in the non-limestone areas of Scotland. The central post in the mortar-mixer would have supported a beam from which a number of paddles were suspended. This would then have been turned by people or animals. The presence of the mortar-mixer and the stone hall reinforces what the historical sources tell us about the site and clearly demonstrates the adoption by the Northumbrians of 'building in the Roman manner'.

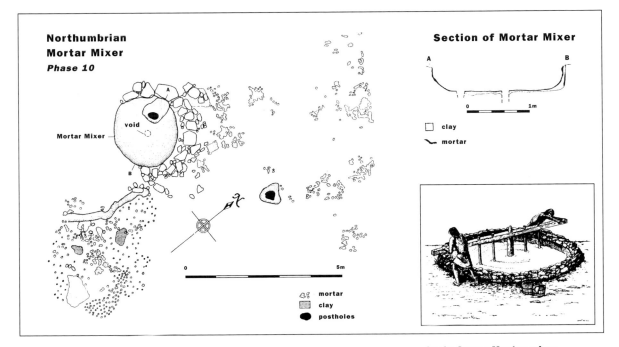

Northumbrian
Mortar Mixer
Phase 10

void

Mortar Mixer

0   5m

mortar
clay
postholes

Section of Mortar Mixer

A   B

0   1m

clay
mortar

Anglo-Saxon Mortar-mixer
Plan and reconstruction of the
Anglo-Saxon mortar-mixer from Dunbar.
SCOTTISH URBAN ARCHAEOLOGICAL TRUST

The display of kingly power

Anglo-Saxon kingship was peripatetic, moving or progressing
from one royal centre or estate to another during the course of
the year. The purpose of the 'progress' would be for the king
to see and be seen, to dispense justice and to reinforce his
authority throughout his domain: it was the exercise of kingly
power outwith the enclosed place. The most admired virtue of
an early king was generosity to his followers. In return, services
and hospitality would have been provided, and tribute in the
form of food collected and consumed. There is no reason to
suppose that British kingship would have been any different.
From the seventh century onwards, the Northumbrian kings
would have had written lists of the services and renders due:
the terms of these conditions will have been set out in charters
and rentals when land-rights (but not necessarily the land itself)
were gifted, appropriated or exchanged. These will have almost
certainly formalised an older, more traditional arrangement of
gift-exchange and other customs.

Although we have some idea of which places would have
been visited, there is little information about how often this
would be, what order the procession would take or whether
certain places were preferred over others at certain times of the

year. Doubtless a set routine would have developed; doubtless some places were preferred above others, whether for the quality of the spread upon the table, the opportunities for hunting, fowling or other sport, or just the chance to meet with old acquaintances. Most people's lives would have been led within the confines of the local township or among its immediate neighbours; kings and their households, like traders, by contrast, would have represented highly mobile elements in an otherwise largely settled population.

Large retinues would accompany the king and his household on what in medieval times would become formalised as royal progresses. Foremost among the group would be

elements of the king's *comitatus*, his bodyguard or war-band. It would probably also include the court bard and almost certainly the royal chaplain, or in earlier times his pagan high-priest (*pontifex*) or wise-man (*magus*). Local officials, left in charge of the king's estates and strongholds, the *villa regia* and *urbs regis* described by Bede and others, would oversee the preparations for the feasts and lodgings: possibly tents or other temporary buildings would have been provided for the lesser members of the party. Two of Ecgfrith's royal officials or reeves, described as *praefectus*, are known to us: Osfrith at Broninis and Tydlin at Dynbaer.

An example of a late seventh-century royal progress through Northumbria, by Ecgfrith and his second wife, Irminburga, is recorded in Eddius

A Royal Progress

The reconstruction drawing shows one of the Northumbrian Bretwaldas (overlords of Britain), possibly Oswiu, in or around 657, coming into one of his royal townships – perhaps Sprouston, near Kelso. Kelso (Calchou) was suggested by the late Dr Ian Smith of the Royal Commission to have been possibly the royal or lordly centre of Cadrod Calchvynyd's kingdom, a lost British kingdom set between Goddeu in Upper Tweeddale and Bernaccia (the predecessor to Anglian Bernicia) to the east.

The king is preceded by his standard-bearer, his bodyguard close at hand; the people come out of their houses to see their king. One of them, a local woman, attracts the attention of her cousin Rhufawn who is part of the king's group. Their ancestors, from further up the Tweed valley, had fought alongside Oswiu's father, Æthelfrith, at the battle of Degsastan: Rhufawn, like his father before him, had been rewarded with the noble title of gesith (king's companion) for their services to the House of Ida. Part of Oswiu's work during the stay will be to confirm some new land grants to Rhufawn's brother, Hewald, and to ride their marches: an old local family had taken the wrong side at the battle of Winwæd (655) and their estates were now to be broken up. Also on the agenda is a troublesome 'rights-of-water' dispute which the local folk-moot has been unable to resolve: to run a new mill that he has just had built, one of Oswiu's gesiths at Simprim has put a dam across a tributary stream which feeds the Leet Water and the folk lower down its course are saying that they have been unable to provide all the necessary flour for the bread which was due under the terms of their land-holding. The problem is exacerbated by the fact that the people at Simprim are one of Oswiu's family's oldest friends whilst the plaintiffs are an old British family of some considerable local influence and importance: they also usually provide some of the best hunting for miles around.

Passing by the small cemetery with its recently completed church, built of timber and thatched with straw, Oswiu and his principal aides are heading for the large building in the centre of the township. This has been made ready for the feast by Aldwin, his praefectus. Tents, to accommodate the musicians and some extra servants who have been brought in for the week-long stay, will be put up in the large open space which fronts onto the king's hall, between it and the cemetery.

CHRIS BROWN

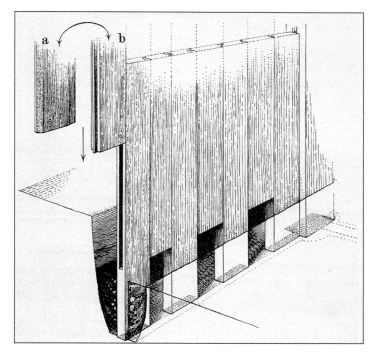

Stephanus' *Life of Wilfrid*: 'the king and queen were making their progress through the cities, forts and townships (*per civitates et castella vicosque*) with worldly pomp and daily feasts and rejoicings'. They were heading for the abbey at Coldingham, probably the site near St Abb's Head, a Northumbrian double-house of monks and nuns and a royal foundation of the 650s. The convent was in the charge of Abbess Æbbe, Ecgfrith's aunt. Incidentally, it was also the place to which Ecgfrith's first wife, Æthelthryth, had retired earlier.

An earlier example of a Northumbrian royal progress, describing Edwin, probably in the late 620s, is recorded by Bede.

Plank Walling
Detail of plank walling in the buildings at Yeavering.
HMSO

*So great was his majesty in his realm that not only were banners carried before him in battle, but even in time of peace, as he rode about among his cities, estates and kingdoms (*civitates, villae, provinciae*) with his thegns, he always used to be preceded by a standard-bearer. Further, when he walked anywhere along the roads, there used to be carried before him the type of standard which the Romans call a* tufa *and the English call a* thuf

The Roman *tufa* has been described as a winged globe mounted on a spear. Its adoption by the kings of Northumbria signifies their self-perception as the heirs of Rome, imbuing their barbarian kingship with the trappings of the Roman Imperial past. Possibly the *tufa* was adopted as the personal standard of the *Bretwalda*, 'Overlord of Britain', an anachronistic title which was bestowed on three of the kings of Northumbria, Edwin, Oswald and Oswiu.

Yeavering: an Anglian Royal township

Perhaps one of the best examples of *romanitas* (the adoption and adaption of things Roman) comes from Yeavering in Northumberland. It was recorded in Bede's History because of a

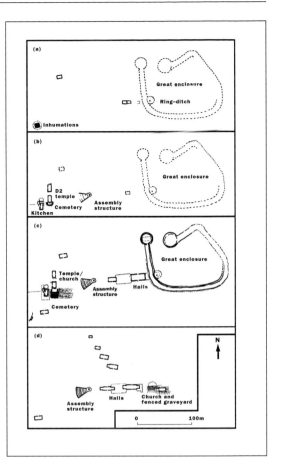

Palace Complex at Yeavering
The development of the Northumbrian palace complex at Yeavering in the sixth and seventh centuries.
N. J. HIGHAM

royal visit to the site, by Edwin, in or around 627. He was accompanied by Paulinus, a significant figure in the conversion of the northern Angles.

Like Dunbar, Yeavering is another high-status Anglian site whose British name, Gefrin, betrays its earlier ancestry. Probably meaning 'The Hill of the Goats', the place-name has been taken as a tribal or totemistic reference to the Iron Age or earlier peoples who gathered in the hillfort of Yeavering Bell, its twin peaks overlooking the later early medieval township to the north.

Yeavering is probably the key excavated site for this period in north Britain. Excavated between 1953 and 1962, it marked a turning point in Anglo-Saxon settlement studies. The site has gone on to give its name to a particular style of building, one constructed with heavy, post- or plank-built load-bearing walls set in a continuous foundation trench, with inclined external buttress-posts and two doors opposite each other in the long walls. Later refinements to the style are represented by the addition of external annexes at one or both ends of the building. Both are now recognised as elements of an early medieval building tradition in widespread use in areas of Anglo-Saxon settlement.

Yeavering is significant for the quality and range of the material remains and for its historical association with the early Northumbrian kings and the Church. It is also important because it is possible to tie down very closely the chronology of the settlement. We know from Bede that the site was 'deserted in the time of the kings who followed Edwin' and the implication is that it had been abandoned long before Bede was writing his History, completed around 731. The excavator of the site, Dr Brian Hope-Taylor, believed that the site's chronology probably extended no later than the times of Oswiu or Ecgfrith, in the 670s or 680s. The opposite end of the chronology, however, is less secure. Controversy surrounds the post-Roman

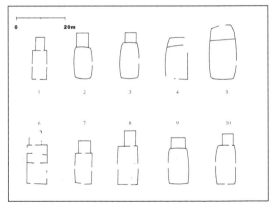

Plans of Timber Halls
Comparative plans of timber halls in Northumbria, East Lothian and Scottish Borders:
I. M. SMITH

(1) Yeavering Bb
(2) Sprouston E1
(3) Thirlings A
(4) Whitekirk B
(5) Whitekirk A
(6) Doon Hill B
(7) Yeavering A1c
(8) Yeavering C4a
(9) Sprouston E2
(10) Yeavering C4b

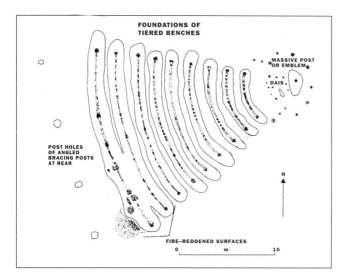

Plan of the Timber Tiered-structure (Grandstand) at Yeavering

N. J. HIGHAM

origins of the township and whether a local native British component can be recognised there in the sixth century. Recent assessments suggest that the architecture of the palisades and the post-built structures from the earliest occupation of the site after Roman times may belong to an Anglian and early medieval building tradition.

During the reign of Edwin in the 620s, the *villa regia* (royal township) of Yeavering saw the construction of one of the most remarkable buildings in post-Roman Britain. Located at a focal point of the township, between a possible pagan temple and cemetery to the west and a large hall and the earlier palisaded fort to the east, was a large, timber tiered-structure or grandstand.

Erected upon nine deep foundation trenches, describing a series of concentric arcs of circles, the building has been likened to a segment of a Roman amphitheatre. Certainly, similar timber structures are known, from both Roman Britain and the continent: one is portrayed on Trajan's Column in Rome. But such parallels are distant both in space and time. The example at Yeavering seems to reflect a local adaptation of a visibly surviving stone example, possibly like those which are known or can be inferred at Catterick or Brough-on-Humber. The Yeavering grandstand, in the words of its excavator, sets upon the township 'the stamp of Rome; blurred and deformed, perhaps, but unmistakable'.

Immediately to the east of the structure was found a group of post-holes, interpreted as a low dais or stage. To either side of and behind the stage, further lines of post-holes may represent the remains of a series of wattle-fences, possibly sounding-boards or screens to make more private the proceedings within. Between the screens and the back of the

stage was a substantial pit, 1.2m deep, in which a vertical post had been erected and subsequently left to rot when the rest of the structure was later dismantled. The post appears to have formed the centre point from which the original front six ranks of the grandstand had been laid out, the rearmost three representing a later extension to the structure. Certain aspects of careful design and planning are also evident in many of the other buildings at Yeavering.

The grandstand has been interpreted as an assembly-place or folk-moot. Possibly this was where Paulinus instructed the people, whom Bede tells us had gathered at Yeavering from all the surrounding villages and countryside, before leading them off to be baptised in the nearby River Glen.

Paulinus, from Rome and a member of the Augustine mission to Kent, had accompanied Edwin and his Kentish queen, Ethelburga, to Yeavering. According to Bede, he spent 36 days there constantly occupied in instruction and baptism. Described as 'tall, with a slight

Reconstruction of the Grandstand at Yeavering
CHRIS BROWN

stoop, black hair, a thin face, a slender aquiline nose ... venerable and awe-inspiring in appearance', Paulinus is one of the few people of this age whose appearance has been recorded in any detail.

Timber forts and the Anglian advance

One of the earliest structures at post-Roman Yeavering was a large palisaded enclosure. Called 'The Great Enclosure', it was considered by its excavator to be a British construction used in connection with livestock, a communal cattle-corral. Others, however, have interpreted it as a fort. Possibly it represents a timber fort or stockade which was thrown up by the Northumbrians in the earliest days of their takeover of Bernicia, added to, repaired and improved in later years, and then abandoned in more settled times. Forts such as these may have been the 'block-houses' of the Anglian advance, the predecessors of the later Norman motte-and-bailey castles, established in strategic areas, on earlier strongholds or at political or ritual centres of power, to dominate, subdue or intimidate those living in the vicinity and to control the major access routes, whether from the sea, between the valleys or along the Roman roads.

Other palisaded enclosures of this period are known from nearby Milfield, from Sprouston and Kirk Hill (near St Abb's Head) in the Scottish Borders and at Doon Hill, near Dunbar (East Lothian). The late reference to the fortification of Bamburgh might be another example. Another site, possibly of this period, has been recognised in the triple-palisaded enclosure at Hogbridge, near Peebles.

In contrast to their buildings and settlements, the 'personal archaeology' of Anglian expansion into southern Scotland, in the form of weapons and the like, is harder to trace. The principal reason for this is the apparent absence of pagan Anglian graves in southern Scotland: none of the large cremation or pagan inhumation cemeteries like those known in Yorkshire has ever been found in Scotland. This lack of evidence is generally attributed to the fact that the initial Anglian invasions only just predate the conversion of the

Cropmarks at Hogbridge, Peebleshire
Aerial photography has revealed cropmark evidence of a triple-palisaded enclosure at Hogbridge, in Peebleshire. It is situated at the edge of a scarp slope above a burn which flows into the Glensax burn just to the east. Roughly D-shaped on plan, the inner palisade encloses an area of about 0.2ha. The site has not been excavated.
RCAHMS

Gold and Garnet Cloisonné Stud
This stud, 2cm in diameter, is part of a
sword harness, from near East Linton
(East Lothian). It was possibly later
reused as a brooch.
NATIONAL MUSEUMS OF SCOTLAND

**Pyramid with Filigree and
Garnet Decoration**
This decorative pyramid, part of a sword
fitting, is from West Craigie farm,
near Dalmeny (West Lothian).
NATIONAL MUSEUMS OF SCOTLAND

kingdom to Christianity.
Pagan graves of this period are
also scarce in Northumberland.
Christian graves, meanwhile,
contained no grave goods.

Few contemporary Anglo-
Saxon weapons of this period
have been found in Scotland:
indeed, Anglo-Saxon artefacts,
in general, are also rare and
what there is tends to be
identified as later Viking
plunder. A possible Anglo-
Saxon spearhead of sixth- or
seventh-century type, now in
Selkirk Museum, is said to
have been found near

Catslackburn in the valley of the Yarrow (Scottish Borders). A gold and garnet cloisonné stud, part of a sword harness, was recently found near East Linton (East Lothian). Probably dating to the early seventh century, this is a fine example of cloisonné work: thin strips of metal, usually gold, are formed into small cells (cloisons), soldered onto a metal base and filled with enamel, glass or precious stones, garnets in this case. Typically associated with the Anglo-Saxon archaeology of Kent and East Anglia, similar objects were also found in the Sutton Hoo ship-burial.

Cropmarks near Tyninghame, East Lothian

These marks describe two large timber hall-like structures, founded on continuous trenches, with a series of rectilinear ditched enclosures to the south. Traces of two smaller buildings (roughly 8m x 4m) are also evident.

RCAHMS

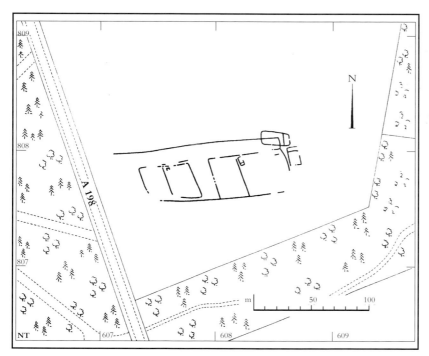

Another sword-fitting was found near Dalmeny (West Lothian) some time before 1853. Previously attributed to Dalmeny churchyard, it is assumed to have been part of a rich Anglo-Saxon warrior-grave but could equally represent a casual loss.

If the palisaded enclosures represent the troubled times of the Anglian takeover of Bernicia, the Borders and Lothian, then the consolidation of that

Cropmarks at Milfield, Northumberland

Mælmin, long recognised as Milfield in Northumberland, lies about two miles north of Yeavering. It has not been excavated. Aerial photography, however, has revealed a palimpsest of fenced-yards, Yeavering-type buildings and Grubenhäuser, together with a massive double-palisaded enclosure. According to Bede, the villa regia at Yeavering was later abandoned and 'another was built instead in a place called Mælmin'.

T. GATES AND C. O'BRIEN

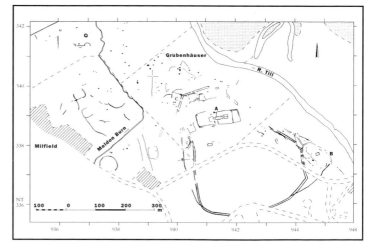

settlement is represented in the townships which grew up outside their walls – townships like those at Yeavering, Milfield and Sprouston.

Place-names

The consolidation of the Anglian hold is also represented in the evidence provided by place-names. In southern Scotland, no less than in Northumbria, place-names formed with *-ingas*, *-ingaham*, *-ingatun* or *-ing* are among the earliest types of Anglo-Saxon names. Existing British settlement names, particularly those relating to earlier centres of power and administration, were also adopted wherever this was convenient and meaningful. Examples would include Gefrin, Mælmin and Dynbaer.

There is an interesting concentration of early Anglo-Saxon place-names in East Lothian. There are three *-ingaham* names: Tyn**inghame**, 'the settlement of the people by the Tyne'; Lyner**yngham**, the old name for East Linton, 'the settlement of the people by the *linn*' (a Brittonic word meaning 'pool'); and Whitt**ingehame**, 'the settlement of the people of Hwita', an Anglo-Saxon personal name. There is also one early example of *-ingatun*: Hadd**ington**, 'the settlement of the people of Hoedda'. Other examples, such as Huntington near Haddington, lack early documentation. Possibly these were the principal settlements of the Northumbrians in the seventh century. That they are of some antiquity is indicated by the fact that all four were of sufficient rank to become centres of parishes: indeed, Tyninghame was the site of a Northumbrian monastery, in place by the eighth century if not earlier. Nearby, aerial photography has revealed the remains of a probable Anglian settlement, possibly a small farmstead attached to the monastery.

Meanwhile, the early importance of Whittingehame may be marked by the dedication of its church to Oswald, saint and former king of Northumbria. The major relics of the saint, his arms and hands, had been enshrined at the cult centre of Bamburgh within a generation of his death in 642. The dedication at Whittingehame would appear to represent an extension of his cult into the newly conquered lands of Northumbria in the latter part of the seventh century.

-ham names, possibly another early naming element, are also well-represented in East Lothian: Mor**ham**, Auld**hame**,

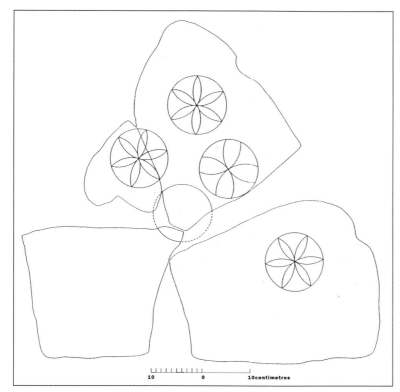

Slab from Whitekirk, East Lothian

This slab, with incised circles of crosses, possibly originally formed one end of a stone shrine. Similar motifs are known from Northumbrian contexts at Whithorn. Examples, however, are also known from much later contexts.

HEADLAND ARCHAEOLOGY

Old**ham**stocks, **Ham**er (the old name for Whitekirk) and the lost Peffer**ham**, preserved now only in the stream-name Pefferburn near Whitekirk, are all located within a few miles of the River Tyne. Another distinctive Anglo-Saxon place-name element is *-bothl*, meaning 'hall', usually of some status. Examples in East Lothian include Eld**botle**, a deserted medieval settlement, near Dirleton, and **Bol**ton, just outside Haddington. Other examples, in south-west Scotland, include **Buittle**, a centre of the medieval lords of Galloway and possibly an earlier centre of Northumbrian defence and administration, and May**bole**, meaning 'hall of the maiden', a parish centre in the medieval period. Its church was dedicated to the Northumbrian saint, Cuthbert, whose cult was fully established by the early eighth century. Fragments of early Northumbrian sculpture are also known from East Lothian: from Aberlady, Morham and Tyninghame. A recently discovered stone describing a series of incised circles of crosses, built into the tithe barn at Whitekirk (East Lothian), might also date to this period.

Northern British timber halls

The use of timber for construction amongst the native northern British peoples is well represented archaeologically, in terms of both timber roundhouses and crannog structures. Few sites in north Britain, however, have produced early rectangular halls which might represent local pre-Anglian constructions. The type is well known in the south and west of England. In north Britain, however, the type has proved elusive.

Two possible key sites emerge. Excavations at Doon Hill, near Dunbar (East Lothian), in the early 1960s revealed the remains of a large rectangular building (Hall A), 23m long and 10.4m wide, with curious V-shaped or 'open-book' gables.

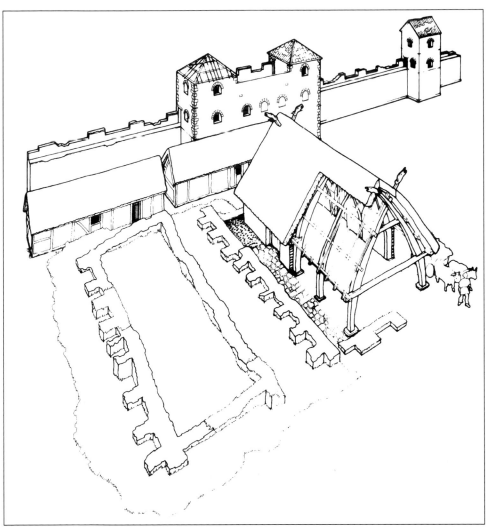

**Early Post-Roman
Timber Halls
from Birdoswald**

Similar in size and plan was a building excavated at Balbridie (Aberdeenshire). Radiocarbon-dating and finds, however, showed that Balbridie had been built 4000 years earlier. As a result, there was a debate over whether the Doon Hill building was also of this date. Its post-Roman credentials, however, have become clear since it is now known that abraded sherds of Roman pottery and ironwork were recovered in the fills of its post-holes. Overlain by a building of mid-seventh-century Yeavering-type (Hall B), the earlier hall is considered by its excavator to have been its fifth- or sixth-century 'British' predecessor.

A series of timber halls, erected within the ruins of the Roman fort of Birdoswald on Hadrian's Wall, have also been assigned a similar date and identified as possibly the halls of a *tyrannus*, one of the local war-lords who assumed power in the aftermath of the withdrawal of Roman troops in the early fifth century. Possibly the petty ruler and the former fort garrison continued to exact their customary tax levies from the local population in return for providing armed protection; possibly it was in sites such as these, as much as in the traditional 'tribal' centres or strongholds, that the foundation stone was laid for the petty lordships and sub-kingdoms of the Early Historic period.

Two substantial post-built halls have also been recorded at Sprouston (near Kelso) and, by analogy with the halls at Birdoswald, it has been said that they could represent native British constructions. Substantial post-built timber halls were also found at Hoddom (Dumfriesshire). Dating to the seventh and eighth centuries and later, it is clear that structures founded on individual earth-fast posts formed part of a common early medieval building tradition, part and parcel of the type of buildings that were being erected in their contemporary Northumbrian heartland.

Three Northern British Timber Halls
Comparative plans of three Northern British timber halls: (a) Doon Hill A; (b) Balbridie; (c) Sprouston.
I. M. SMITH

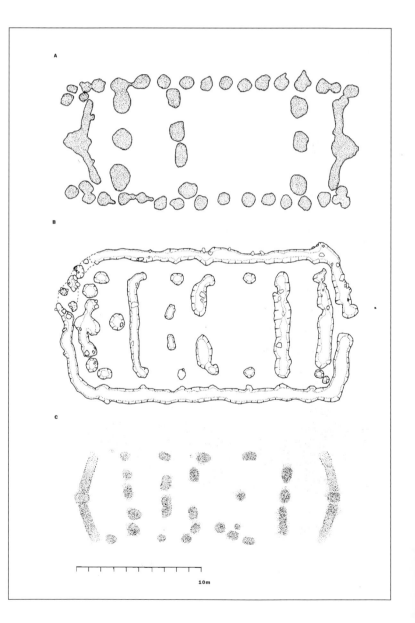

Stones, Shrines and Cemeteries

Christianity, a literate religion, was the principal means by which the legacy of the country's Roman past was preserved. Its churchmen not only compiled all manner of ecclesiastical documents, such as gospels, commentaries, hymnals and histories, but were also the civil servants of the time – the successors in some ways of the Roman civil administration – involved in the writing, for example, of legal titles and processes, writs and laws. Some of the writings from this very early period survive, as

The Viventius & Mavorius Stone, Kirkmadrine (Dumfries & Galloway)
HISTORIC SCOTLAND

The Florentius Stone, Kirkmadrine (Dumfries & Galloway)
HISTORIC SCOTLAND

Patrick and Gildas

The writings both of Patrick, for the fifth century, and of Gildas for the sixth, reveal their grounding in a classical Late Roman education of grammar and rhetoric. Training in rhetoric was the mainstay of a traditional Roman education, for its civil servants, administrators and lawyers. Both Patrick's *Confession* and *Letter* and Gildas' tirade against Britain's tyrants and corrupt priests are structured in accordance with a model of rhetoric whose precise rules were laid down in a series of manuals and treatises on the subject. Typically, the piece would comprise the *exordium* (introduction), the *narratio* (narrative historical background to the case), the *propositio* (outline), the *argumentatio* (detail), followed by the *anacephalaeosis* (summing-up) and the *epilogus*, in which the sympathies of the audience would be finally appealed to.

The evidence of Patrick's writing suggests that rhetorical schools were still flourishing in Britain, as on the continent, during the first half of the fifth century: Gildas' writings show that rhetorical training, if not necessarily in schools, was still available some hundred years later.

Both Patrick and Gildas have been seen as northern Britons. Indeed, later hagiography – *The Life of Gildas*, written in the eleventh century – makes Gildas a north Briton of Pictish ancestry. Certainly, there is a northern perspective in his writing: his (erroneous) accounts of the two Roman walls (Hadrian and Antonine) which were built to protect the province, his concern with the raiding Irish and Picts and his account that the first Saxon mercenaries, brought in to stem this northern menace, were settled 'on the east side of the island', an action which would only make sense if the north-east of England or south-east Scotland was meant. Possibly this is an allusion to a story, related in the *Historia Brittonum*, that Ochta and Ebissa, with forty keels, were given land 'in the north about the Wall ... as far as the borders of the Picts', presumably Lothian. Chester and Carlisle (and even Strathclyde, though this seems unlikely) have been suggested as possible places of composition. The northern bias and the inferred northern setting for Gildas are not, however, shared by all scholars, and a place of writing in south-west England or Wales can also be proposed. With Patrick, on the other hand, there does seem to be an emerging consensus for a northern origin.

Patrick, originally called Sochet or Succetus, was a Briton. Whatever his exact dates, there is a general consensus that he lived and worked wholly within the fifth century, dying as an old man perhaps in the 490s. His father Calpurnius was or had been both *diaconus* (a Christian deacon) and *decurio* (a Roman civil administrator). His grandfather, Potitus, had been a *presbyter* (priest). Patrick himself was successively a deacon and bishop. Some of these offices and grades are known from early inscribed stones of this period, both from southern Scotland and elsewhere.

Clearly, with three generations of churchmen in the family, as well as an office in a late- or sub-Roman civil hierarchy, Patrick's family was of some social standing and importance. The family owned a small estate (*villula*), with servants, near a place called *vicus bannavem taburniae*, a corruption it has been suggested of *Bannaventa Berniae*. This has been identified with *Banna*, the Roman fort of Birdoswald, or *Glannoventa*, the Roman fort at Ravenglass on the Cumbrian coast. It was there that Patrick, along with the family servants, was captured by an Irish slave-raiding party and taken to Ireland.

The significance of Patrick's and Gildas' writings is that they clearly describe, for the later fifth and mid-sixth centuries respectively, a still-functioning ecclesiastical hierarchy and some form of literate 'Roman' administration. Their possible northern perspective then raises the possibility that there was an organised Church which could continue to maintain or introduce Christianity among the peoples of southern Scotland at this time.

manuscripts (whether in their original form or as later, medieval copies) and as inscriptions on stone.

The development of early Christianity in southern Scotland operated within the framework provided by the emerging British kingdoms, themselves based to a greater or lesser extent, as we have seen, on much older tribal groupings. There is also some evidence to suggest that this Church, in terms of its organisation and structure, was based on territorial dioceses, in the charge of bishops. Archaeological evidence for Christianity in southern Scotland between the Antonine Wall and Hadrian's Wall in the fifth and sixth centuries is principally represented by a series of inscribed memorial stones. Composed in Latin and containing both British and Roman personal names, these stones show a sub-Roman Church whose texts continued to be composed in Latin and, as Professor Charles Thomas has pointed out, whose officials continued to speak, read and probably write in Latin to a far greater extent than is generally recognised.

The earliest inscribed stones appear in the south-west of the country, from Whithorn and Kirkmadrine. They can be approximately dated by the style of their lettering, by the linguistic forms of some of the British personal names which appear on them and with reference to the stylistic evolution of the chi-rho motif, an early Christian motif formed from the first two Greek letters in the name *Christos*, 'The Anointed One'.

The so-called Latinus stone, from Whithorn, is generally considered to be the earliest post-Roman inscribed stone in Scotland, possibly dating to around the middle of the fifth century. It is usually assumed to have been a tombstone. Set below a very faint Constantinian six-armed chi-rho motif, the inscription is traditionally

Roman Inscriptions, Hoddom
Two fragmentary Roman inscriptions built into the early building at Hoddom (Dumfries & Galloway).
HISTORIC SCOTLAND

The Latinus Stone, Whithorn (Dumfries & Galloway)
This stone, with its chi-rho motif now restored, was recovered during excavations at the end of the nineteenth century, possibly from the area of the north transept of the medieval priory church.
CHARLES THOMAS

translated as: We, Latinus, 35 years, and his daughter, 4 years, praise the Lord. The grandson, Barrovadus, set up this memorial. An alternative interpretation, viewing the slab not as a memorial stone but as a dedication slab, has been put forward by Professor Charles Thomas: We praise thee Lord. Latinus, 35 years, and his daughter, 4 years, here in this place made a *sinus*. He (Latinus) was a grandson/descendant of Barrovadus. The Latin word *sinus*, with the abstract meaning of 'shelter' or 'refuge', may represent an Early Christian synonym for 'church'. It has been suggested that possibly the stone originally stood outside the entrance of a mid-fifth-century church on the site, newly-founded by its aristocratic patron, Latinus.

From Kirkmadrine on the Rhinns peninsula there is a group of slightly later inscribed memorial stones, probably dating to the early 500s. With known continental prototypes, this group of stones may reflect contacts with Gaul at this period. One of them commemorates Viventius and Mavorius, two 'holy and outstanding' *sacerdotes* (priests). One, partly damaged, names a certain Florentius. Another from the Rhinns, now lost, is reported to have borne an inscription to Ventidius, a sub-deacon (*subdiaconus*).

These inscriptions are significant for two main reasons. Firstly, their literary formulas and motifs imply connections with Gaul and the wider continent or Mediterranean area. The stones reflect the contacts shown by the pieces of imported pottery and sherds of glass vessels which archaeologists have recognised on an increasing number of sites throughout the Irish Sea area, including Whithorn itself and, as we have seen, Alt Clut, which stands at the northern end of this early trade nexus.

Secondly, the stones have much to tell us about the structure of the early Church. The references from the Rhinns to *sacerdotes* (priests) and a sub-deacon, like others from Peebles in the east, one commemorating a *sacerdos* named as Neitano and another (now lost) seemingly referring to a *diaconus*, bring to mind the ecclesiastical grades which are referred to in Patrick's writings. They appear to

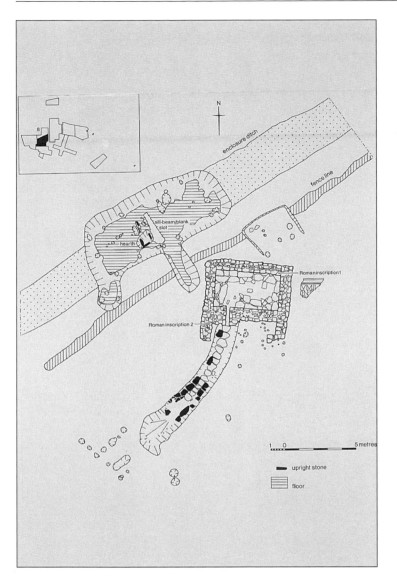

The Possible Baptistery at Hoddom (Dumfries & Galloway)
Plan and photograph of the possible baptistery at Hoddom, showing later features to the north.

indicate that an organised, hierarchical Church was (still) operating in southern Scotland down to the middle of the sixth century at least.

Baptism and buildings of the early British Church

Evidence from Hoddom (Dumfriesshire) might suggest that the sub-Roman British Church was still functioning as late as the end of the sixth century. An early detached building there, dating to around 600 and buried beneath the bank of the Northumbrian enclosure, has been identified as a possible baptistery. Such a structure, if correctly interpreted, would indicate the existence of

Kentigern Performs his Last Baptism

Kentigern, old and frail, his lower jaw bandaged to prevent any unseemly gaping of his
mouth (as described in his Life), is aided as he performs his last baptism.
CHRIS BROWN

a still-functioning ecclesiastical hierarchy which could appoint officials and organise its affairs.

Baptism represents the most fundamental of all Christian rituals: symbolically it represents both the death of the individual and his spiritual rebirth into everlasting life. The archaeology and architecture of baptism thus share many of the aspects of death, burial and the tomb. The pre-enclosure building at Hoddom, possibly a baptistery, was oriented east–west and comprised both an above- and a below-ground element. The subterranean part of the building had been erected inside a large subrectangular pit, at the corner of which was a contemporary drain or soak-away containing deposits of charcoal and lime. Both the pit and the soak-away were paved and luted with clay. Built of Roman masonry (robbed from the nearby Roman fort at Birrens) the walls of the sunken chamber were also packed with clay and constructed on top of the floor. The superstructure of the building is reconstructed as a clay and timber building, resting on oak sill-beams, its walls washed or rendered with lime. Clearly, the building was of some sophistication and, when freshly washed with lime, would have been a conspicuous feature of the local landscape – a 'white-house', a symbolically appropriate colour for a baptistery, reflecting the process of purification and the white robes in which the newly baptised were dressed. Water was presumably brought to the building by hand from the nearby spring. The sunken part of the building may have been filled with water: alternatively, perhaps a wooden or lead-tank was placed over a low platform in the centre of the sunken room.

The late Monsignor David McRoberts has argued that the episode in a twelfth-century *Life of St Kentigern*, concerning the holy man's death, represents a garbled account of his last baptismal service, Kentigern collapsing during the ceremony and dying eight days later.

> *When the octave of the Lord's Epiphany [i.e. 13 January], on which the gentle bishop himself had been wont every year to wash a multitude of people in sacred baptism, was dawning … the holy man, borne by their hands, entered a vessel filled with hot water, which he had first blessed with the sign of salvation; and a circle of the brethren standing round him, awaited the issue of the event.*
> Jocelyn, Life of St Kentigern, *ch. 44*

The reconstruction painting shows this possible baptismal scene, using for its setting the early sunken building at Hoddom.

There is also a suggestion that a series of apse-ended buildings on native Romano-British settlements might represent possible church buildings, including one on Traprain Law (East Lothian).

Round-ended Buildings on Native Sites

Round-ended buildings from northern Britain, compared with a reconstruction of a late fourth century apsidal church from Icklingham (Suffolk): (1) Traprain Law (East Lothian); (2) Cow Green (Cumbria); (3) Glencoyndale (Cumbria); (4) The Dod (Scottish Borders); (5) Huckhoe (Northumberland); (6) Icklingham (Suffolk).
I. M. SMITH

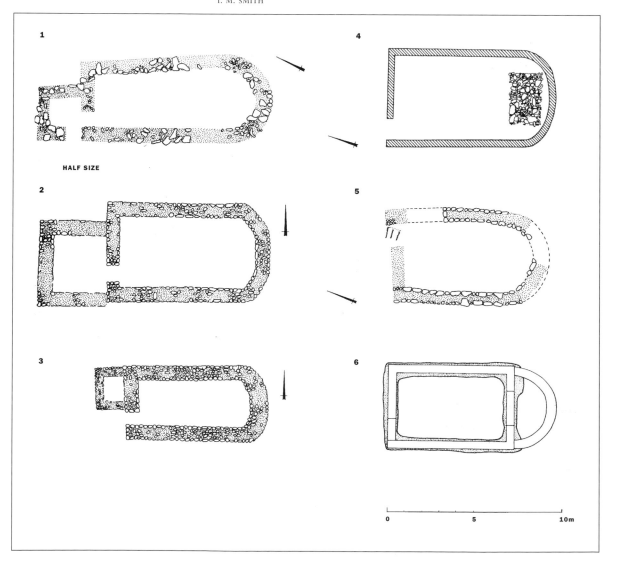

Eccles place-names

Early British ecclesiastical centres might also be represented by the distribution of the *eccles* place-names. These have long been recognised as a potentially early, British sub-Roman place-name element for denoting Christian settlements or churches. Generally, the place-name has been considered as an active naming element appropriate to the fifth century or possibly slightly later in north Britain between the Roman Walls. The ultimate source of the word is Latin *ecclesia*, meaning 'church'. To some scholars, these place-names have been taken to signify the former presence of British or Romano-British church buildings; to others, the term has been interpreted as referring to a Christian congregation or community. It is, of course, very different from the Anglo-Saxon or Germanic word for church, *cirice*, and the place-name, to have had meaning, must have been given by native British speakers.

The distribution of *eccles* place-names in England is

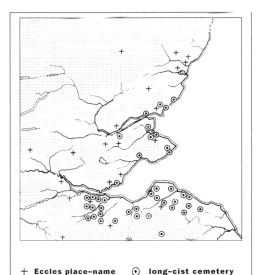

+ **Eccles place-name** ⊙ **long-cist cemetery**

Distribution Map
Distribution of long-cist cemeteries and eccles place-names in south-east Scotland.

Long-cist Cemetery, The Catstane, Midlothian
Part of the long-cist cemetery at The Catstane. Radiocarbon dates from the cemetery indicate that it flourished in the period 485–660.
HISTORIC SCOTLAND

predominantly western and north-western, those very areas which remained in British hands down to at least the later fifth century. The distribution is also continued into southern Scotland. Included among these are three simplex Eccles names, one near Stirling and others in Berwickshire and Dumfriesshire, and several compound forms: Egglesbrec, near Falkirk, Eaglesham south of Glasgow, Ecclesmachan in West Lothian, Eaglescairnie in East Lothian and Ecclefechan, near Hoddom in Dumfriesshire.

The recent excavations at Hoddom might help throw some light on the date, age and significance of the *eccles* place-names. The small village of Ecclefechan, meaning 'little church', lies just a few kilometres to the north of the Anglian monastery and the site of the later, medieval parish church of Hoddom. Possibly the large monastic enclosure there was the original Eccles? Ecclefechan, in other words, may have been named to distinguish it from the much larger settlement nearby. However, if so, then this would almost certainly imply the presence of a predominantly Brittonic-speaking local population. This, then, might raise the possibility that the excavated settlement, if known locally as Eccles, may have always been known to its inhabitants by the Anglo-Saxon place-name of Hoda's Elm, first recorded in the twelfth century as Hodelme (Hoddom); some such scenario might explain the survival of the

Antiquarian Drawing of The Catstane
A large rounded boulder, possibly a prehistoric standing stone later reused. Carved on one face in debased Roman capitals, possibly of late fifth or early sixth century date, is an inscription. It reads: 'In this tomb lies Vetta, daughter of Victricius'. Many early Christian cemeteries were established on earlier sacred sites.
SOCIETY OF ANTIQUARIES OF SCOTLAND

Hoddom nomenclature and the disappearance of an original Eccles, preserved only by implication as a fossil element in the surviving place-name Ecclefechan.

The antiquity of the name at Hoddom and its ascription to the Northumbrian-period settlement might also be reflected in the fact that Hoddom was almost certainly a *matrix ecclesia*, a 'mother- or head-church' of a locality. When the church at Hoddom was transferred to the jurisdiction of Glasgow in the early twelfth century, it headed a list of churches in Annandale, almost certainly its dependent daughter-houses.

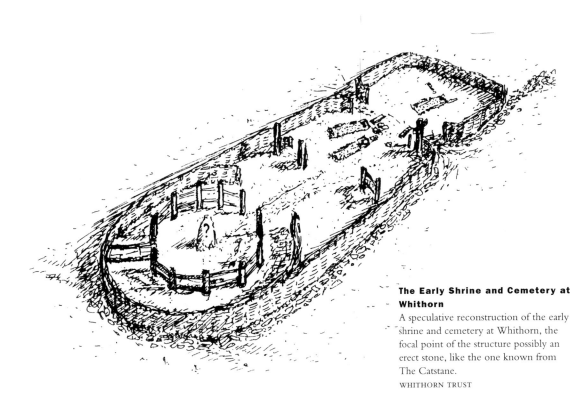

The Early Shrine and Cemetery at Whithorn

A speculative reconstruction of the early shrine and cemetery at Whithorn, the focal point of the structure possibly an erect stone, like the one known from The Catstane.
WHITHORN TRUST

Long-cist cemeteries

Other aspects of Christianity at this period are represented archaeologically by a large number of cemeteries of long stone-lined graves (cists). Many are known in Lothian and Fife. Some, such as the Catstane, beside the runway at Edinburgh Airport, appear to have been focused on an earlier standing stone; there are hints that others may have been established on earlier sacred or ritual sites.

Both stone cists – stone boxes formed of split stones set on edge and covered with a lid of one or more flat stones – and log coffins were present among the earliest graves at Whithorn. Semi-circular log coffins, or possibly leather coffins, have also been recognised in recent excavations of a long-cist cemetery at Thornybank, near Dalkeith (Midlothian). Possibly the most famous recipient of a log-coffin was Bridei, the Pictish king who overthrew Ecgfrith's army at Nechtansmere in 685. An early Irish elegy records his burial in 'a block of hollow withered oak'.

Radiocarbon dating suggests that long-cist cemeteries flourished from the late fifth to the mid- seventh century. They represent the earliest field monuments of the sub-Roman Church in the north. Some, perhaps, were subsequently 'developed' by the addition of open-air shrines and churches. The apparent abandonment of many during the course of the seventh century may reflect a movement away from places of local burial towards burial at what would, over time, come to be the parish centres of the district. Possibly this change was brought about as a result of the Northumbrian takeover.

The inscribed stones, the long-cist cemeteries, shrines and other ritual buildings, the eccles settlements: this was the ecclesiastical landscape which the Northumbrians invaded and which they would mould to their own needs.

Enclosed Places: Centres of Spiritual and Economic Power

Aerial View of Kirkhill, near St Abbs Head (Scottish Borders)

RCAHMS

The Northumbrian settlement of earlier, secular places of power and administration may be paralleled by their similar takeover of ecclesiastical centres. Secular and ecclesiastical conquest went hand-in-hand. For example, Wilfrid, the powerful late-seventh-century Northumbrian bishop, had ecclesiastical dominion over 'the British, Scots and Picts to the north' as far as the bounds of the Northumbrian kingdom itself. According to his biographer, in a speech which was delivered on the steps of his newly completed church at Ripon in the 670s, he also had a list of the 'holy places in various parts of the country which the British clergy, fleeing from our own hostile sword, had deserted'. Perhaps these were places like the Thornybank long-cist cemetery, like Hoddom, or Traprain.

Bede tells us of four early monastic foundations which were established in southern Scotland by the Northumbrians: Whithorn, Abercorn, Old Melrose and St Æbbe's monastery which was established at a place called Urbs Coludi. The same place is referred to by other contemporary writers as Colodesbyrig and Colodaesburg, meaning 'Colud's fort'. All four sites are the sites of earlier, British foundations.

Æbbe's monastery has been identified as Kirk Hill, near St Abb's Head, Coldingham: a double-monastery (housing both men and women), it was probably founded in the 650s. The story of its destruction by fire in the 680s and its subsequent abandonment was related to Bede by Eadgisl, a monk who had been living in the monastery at the time. Seemingly burned down through some unspecified act of carelessness, the destruction of its lofty buildings, both communal and private, is described as a divine punishment for turning a place of prayer into 'haunts of feasting, drinking, gossip and other delights'.

The turf-covered remains of the medieval church and its graveyard lie close to the edge of the cliffs. The landward side of the headland is marked by a broad rampart, about 8m wide and 3m high. Sectioning of the rampart revealed evidence for an earlier palisaded enclosure of the promontory. Radiocarbon dating of one of the palisades suggests that the headland was probably first enclosed in the 600s. Possibly this was the original fort of Colodaesburg, the later turf and clay rampart being the vallum of Æbbe's monastery.

British ecclesiastical credentials are clearest in the case of Whithorn (Bede's Candida Casa) associated with the Romano-British saint, St Ninian, in the fifth or sixth century. Clearly part of Bernicia when Bede was writing, the church at Whithorn was raised to the status of a bishopric under Pechthelm some time in the early 700s, 'the number of believers having so increased of late'. Peter Hill's recent excavations there have thrown much light on the development of the site, from its earliest post-Roman beginnings down to the period of the Northumbrian settlement and beyond.

Restored Cross-fragments from Abercorn, West Lothian
Reconstruction of the front and side views of the restored cross-fragments from Abercorn.
SOCIETY OF ANTIQUARIES OF SCOTLAND

Timber Church and Chapel from Whithorn
Reconstruction of the axially-aligned timber church and burial chapel from Northumbrian Whithorn, circa 800, with rows of ancillary buildings below.
WHITHORN TRUST

This is a view of the Northumbrian monastery at Hoddom as it might have been at its height, maybe around 800. In the foreground is the ferryman, one of the monastery's lay dependants: his family have worked the land hereabouts for generations. In the centre ground, the funeral of one of the monastic brethren is taking place: an old man, he had been the singing master. Having been trained in the church music and chants which were brought to all the Northumbrian churches at the time of Bishop Wilfrid and Eddius Stephanus some hundred years before, he had gone on to teach psalmody and chants to several generations of younger scholars and priests at Hoddom. As a mark of respect he is accorded a place of rest on the south side of the cross. Local tradition among the brethren might have suggested that this marks the site of one of St Kentigern's miracles. To the west of the cross is the principal monastic church: directly to the east, is a second, smaller church which is also used as a mausoleum for the principal office-holders and the family of the foundation's aristocratic patrons. The presence of axially aligned churches is a well-documented feature of Northumbrian monasteries. Examples are known from Whithorn and elsewhere.

Outside the ecclesiastical centre of the monastery, represented by its churches and cemetery, are the communal sleeping-quarters, kitchens, the infirmary and other buildings. The guest-house, perhaps, lies to the north-west, near the entrance through the great enclosure. The ancillary agricultural buildings are located on the upper terrace. Overseen by the monastic cellarer, these buildings are the economic power-houses of the settlement, producing income in kind both for the monastery and for its secular patrons.
CHRIS BROWN

Cross fragment from Hoddom
One of many cross fragments recovered during deep ploughing of the lower field. Their distribution indicates that the monastic cemetery lay in the area between the two churches.
HISTORIC SCOTLAND

A Cross from Hoddom, on Discovery and after Cleaning
HISTORIC SCOTLAND

Cross–base, Hoddom
The cross-base, socketed on top, is now rolled up against the east side of the modern graveyard.
HISTORIC SCOTLAND

Both Abercorn (Æbbercurnig) and Old Melrose (Mailros) were Anglo-Saxon monasteries in the seventh century. Both are British topographical place-names. Like Luel, derived from the Romano-British name for Carlisle (Luguvalium) and also the site of a Northumbrian monastery at this time, the continued use of these non-Anglo-Saxon names may suggest the takeover of earlier, sub-Roman, British ecclesiastical centres.

Old Melrose, occupying a promontory site in a bend of the River Tweed, was the place in which St Cuthbert, later bishop of Lindisfarne (died 687), received his monastic instruction and training. The site, unexcavated, is enclosed on one side by a substantial bank and ditch, the monastic vallum (enclosure), which extends across the neck of the promontory.

Abercorn, near the eastern end of the Antonine Wall, was the site of a Northumbrian bishopric where Trumwine was sent by archbishop Theodore of York in 681, as bishop to the English settlements in Lothian. Limited excavations outside the modern graveyard revealed fragments of what may be part of the monastic vallum. Sherds of seventh-century Gaulish table-ware were also reportedly found. The monastery at Abercorn was apparently abandoned in the aftermath of the Northumbrian defeat at Nechtansmere in 685, Trumwine retiring to the royal monastery at Whitby. The presence at the site of fragments of an Anglian-style cross-shaft, probably dating to the eighth or ninth centuries, however, clearly testifies to the continued occupation or re-occupation of the site in later times.

The Northumbrian takeover of earlier, British ecclesiastical sites works at two levels. Certainly, it would have been partly a question of land and resources. The religious establishments themselves and their dependent churches and other land-holdings, as well as the dues and services which went with the land, would have been significant acquisitions in their own right.

The Post-medieval and Modern Graveyard at Hoddom

The graveyard at Hoddom, from the west. The site of the church lies in the north-east corner of the graveyard. Outside, to the west, are a series of crop-marks defining a rectilinear layout, aligned north-west to south-east. Just beyond these is the pronounced mark of the enclosure ditch, together with an entrance gap. The enclosure ditch can also be seen on the upper river terrace, beyond the trees. This was the site of the 1991 excavation.

RCAHMS

But, in an age of belief, there were also less tangible considerations. Monasteries at this time, and indeed throughout the medieval period, were the spiritual 'power-houses', the points of material contact with the unseen world. The appropriation of a local saint's cult would be particularly important to the new rulers.

At Whithorn, and possibly at Hoddom too, there is evidence to suggest that the Northumbrians adopted and developed the cults of St Ninian and St Kentigern. Both were local British saints of some standing. Both possessed quasi-Roman credentials in the sense that both could be construed as the inheritors of the Roman Church in Britain. Indeed, the very great age which is attributed to Kentigern – he is said to have been 185 years old at his death in 612 – may reflect a literary convention to link

Excavations at Hoddom
Excavations on the upper terrace (centre of picture) in 1991. Modern graveyard in foreground.
HISTORIC SCOTLAND

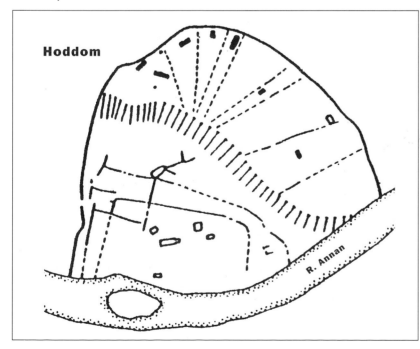

Plan of the Monastery at Hoddom
A reconstruction plan of the Northumbrian monastery at Hoddom, showing the internal division of the site and the distribution of known (blocked) or inferred (open) buildings.

Perimeter Buildings at Hoddom
Detail of some of the perimeter buildings
at Hoddom: a sunken corn-drying kiln at
centre and the outline of a kiln-barn to
right. The broad dark line just to the
north is the fill of the enclosure ditch.
The buildings, set into the bank, were
built up against the palisade.
HISTORIC SCOTLAND

him with that earlier time. The Northumbrian adoption of these
British saints could have also been a means of legitimising their
conquest. It is not without significance, for example, that the
Bernician royal line could claim some degree of kinship with
Kentigern (ostensibly a grandson of Urien) as a result of the
marriage of Oswiu and Rieinmellt, a princess of the House of
Rheged and great-grand-daughter of Urien. The inclusion of yet
another saint in the extended Bernician dynasty (in addition to
Oswiu's brother, St Oswald, and later his sister, St Æbbe) –
particularly one who was a local Northern British aristocrat with
a link, however tenuous, to the Roman past – could well have
aided the Northumbrian takeover of Rheged.

The Anglo-Saxon *villa regiae*, such as the townships of
Yeavering, Milfield and Sprouston, no less than the large
monastic enclosures like the one revealed by excavation at
Hoddom, were also economic 'power-houses'. The site at
Hoddom was bounded by a large curvilinear enclosure, set
around a bend on the north bank of the River Annan.
Excavation on the upper terrace revealed the remains of the
enclosure ditch and palisade, together with a series of ancillary
buildings, mostly corn-drying kilns and barns. The rest of the
reconstruction plan (previous page) is based on crop-mark
evidence, geophysical survey and field-walking after ploughing.

Occupying the same landscape and involved in the

(a)

(b)

(c)

(d)

exploitation of the same agricultural economy, it is not surprising that these secular and ecclesiastical settlements should come to resemble each other. Indeed, there are very real difficulties in distinguishing monastic houses of this period from contemporary high-status secular settlements with attached churches and graveyards. The intensive agricultural regime evident at Hoddom would not be out of place at somewhere like Sprouston or Milfield.

These were some of the largest enclosed places in north Britain at the time. The enclosed area at Hoddom (18ha), for example, is of a similar size to that on Iona; those at Kirk Hill, St Abbs (3ha), Sprouston (0.75ha) or Yeavering (0.75ha), by comparison, are significantly smaller. Only the extremely large palisaded enclosure at Milfield/Maelmin (12ha) comes close. Significantly, however, none of these places developed into the commercial towns of the medieval period. Indeed, of all the known Northumbrian centres in southern Scotland, it seems that only Whithorn and Dunbar made the vital step from *villa regia* or monastery to medieval urban centre.

Trade elsewhere at this time in the Anglian-settled areas of southern Scotland seems to have been restricted to occasional local markets. The reconstruction painting on pages 58-9 shows an early Northumbrian trading site in East Lothian. Possibly it is the beach below Tyninghame or Aberlady. Both places have produced Anglian sculpture and are potentially prime sites for Northumbrian settlement in the area; a fine collection of Anglo-Saxon metalwork has also recently come to light in Aberlady. Perhaps it is a local saint's festival, possibly St Baldred's at Tyninghame. Pilgrims have come to his shrine; goods and services have been brought in from the surrounding district and from as far as Fife. The temporary market, located on the beach below the church, would have been regulated by the king's ealdorman or reeve or possibly by the Church itself. Important but low-level economic activity such as this, however, leaves little archaeological trace.

Metalwork from Aberlady
Late eighth or ninth-century Anglo-Saxon metalwork from Aberlady (East Lothian).
(a) Head (27mm diameter) of copper-alloy disc-headed pin, with traces of gilding. Openwork interlaced animal ornament, with point of attachment with shaft visible at bottom.
(b) Copper alloy strap-end, 44mm long.
(c) Fragmentary copper-alloy mount (38mm long) with cast animal interlace decoration.
(d) Polygonal-headed pin fragment (37mm long) with incised dot and circle design on the facets. Copper-alloy with traces of inlay.
NATIONAL MUSEUMS OF SCOTLAND

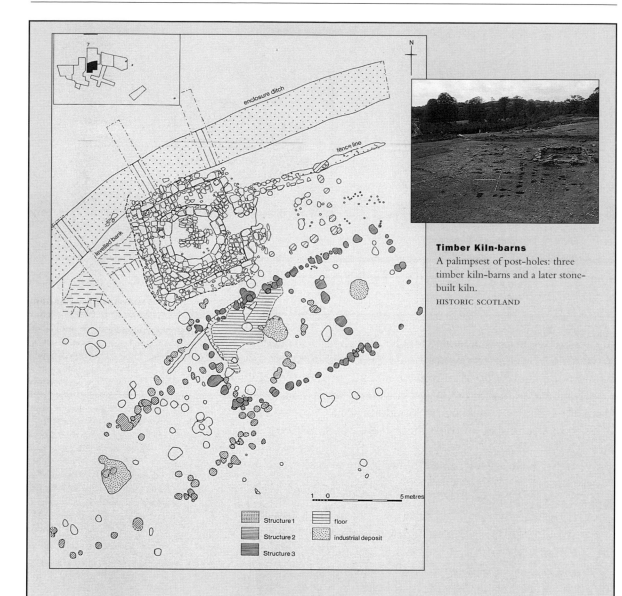

enclosure ditch

fence line

levelled bank

N

Timber Kiln-barns

A palimpsest of post-holes: three timber kiln–barns and a later stone-built kiln.

HISTORIC SCOTLAND

1 0   5 metres

Structure 1   floor

Structure 2   industrial deposit

Structure 3

Grain-drying

Excavations at Hoddom have revealed the remains of several contemporary corn-drying kilns or kiln-barns. All were built of wood, only their post-holes remaining. Some were later built of timber on a stone foundation. The buildings were located around the monastic enclosure. The position of the buildings would seem to suggest that the potential fire-hazard that these buildings posed was fully appreciated by their builders. Nonetheless, each of these buildings burned down at least once.

The relationship between a grain of oats or a head of wheat and something like the Lindisfarne Gospels or the Ruthwell Cross may not be immediately apparent. Yet it was in buildings like those at Hoddom that the primary produce of a monastery and its land was translated into the wealth that produced the illuminated manuscripts, the fine metalwork or pieces of sculpture which were produced in the Northumbrian and other monastic houses of this time. Humble corn-drying kilns like these were the engines of the monastic revolution, which witnessed a level of economic production and

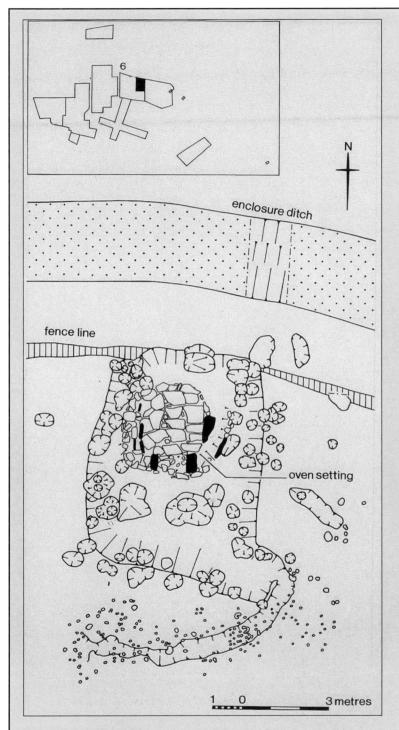

Plan of Corn-drying Kiln

Plan of sunken corn-drying kiln, with protruding entrance at one corner. The building was probably originally constructed within the thickness of the enclosure bank.

organisation which had not been seen since the collapse of Roman Britain.

Five different types of kiln have been recognised at Hoddom. These possibly reflect technological developments and changing economic circumstances over time. The earliest type was no more than a shallow clay-lined pit, about 1.5m across, over which was constructed a wooden superstructure formed of wattle and clay. Something of the sort is described in *The Life of St Ciaran* (an early Irish saint and contemporary of Columba), where corn-drying was undertaken in a round wattle structure set in sand or possibly clay over a fire in the barn.

Oats were the principal crop which was dried in the kilns at Hoddom; there were lesser but regularly occurring quantities of barley and rye. Wheat was very rare over most of the site but in one of the kilns it was the dominant cereal. Significantly, weed seed found with the wheat was atypical of the other grain collections recovered, indicating that the wheat had been grown on less acid soils. This may suggest that either the wheat was imported or it represents a short-lived experiment at local cultivation in what, for wheat, would be an unfavourable climate. Possibly, it represents part of a 'monastic package' which the Northumbrian farmers brought with them from their English homeland.

Reconstruction of an East Lothian Temporary Market

CHRIS BROWN

Kiln-barn at Hoddom
One of the kiln-barns, its outline indicated by its post-holes.
HISTORIC SCOTLAND

Tending the Kiln
Tending the kiln in one of the kiln-barns at Hoddom. Note the pile of clay to the right of the kiln, used to repair it after firing.
CHRIS BROWN

The reconstruction drawing shows one of the later kiln-types at Hoddom, set at the far end of the kiln-barn shown in the photograph. The kiln comprises a wattle-and-daub structure set over a stone base and fired from a stone box, slightly sunk into the ground. The grain is laid on sacking over a wooden mesh. The kiln would need to be tended throughout the drying operation; to turn the grain and to feed and control the fire.

Conclusions

There are perhaps few individual places in southern Scotland today where the country's sub-Roman, British and Anglian pasts come together. Whithorn is one example but probably the best single place from which to view this past would be Traprain Law: not only the site itself, which was possibly in use in the earliest part of this period, but the places that can be seen from it. There are the Castle Rock and Arthur's Seat in Edinburgh to the west, the hills of Fife and the Firth of Forth (the 'sea of Iudeu') to the north, and the landscape of East Lothian all around. It was also a place from which coastal traffic coming up from Bamburgh and Lindisfarne to the south and east could be monitored.

The immediate landscape has obviously changed much in the thousand years and more since the armies of Yrfai, Urien, Oswald, Oswiu and Ecgfrith passed by its foot, or since Trumwine and his priests fled south to Whitby from Abercorn in the aftermath of the defeat at Nechtansmere. Yet the settlements of the Britons and the early Northumbrians are still there, fossilised in the place-names. This is the landscape of Scotland before the Scots when the everyday speech of the field, market place or township would have been Brittonic or a northern Anglian dialect of Old English.

The days when a 'Welshman' or a 'Yorkshireman' or a 'Northumbrian' ruled the roost from Castle Rock, Edinburgh, are long gone. However, through the Church and their secular institutions, with links going back to the last days of Roman Britain, the Britons and Angles of 1500 years ago are an essential element in the forging of the medieval Scottish nation.

Sites Around Scotland

A number of the sites listed below are opened to the public by Historic Scotland (HS) or other agencies (P), but many are in private ownership and permission should be sought from the owner before making a visit; due care should of course be taken to avoid damage to the monument and any personal injury arising from, for example, rough or uneven ground. The sites are grouped alphabetically in local authority areas, with Ordnance Survey grid references indicating their location.

Angus

Aberlemno churchyard: class II Pictish symbol stone, with battle scene, possibly commemorating Ecgfrith's defeat at Nechtansmere.
NO 522 558

Nechtansmere/Dunnichen Moss: the site of the Northumbrian defeat at the hands of the Picts and Britons. No archaeological remains of the battle have ever been recovered and its precise site is not known. There is, however, a confused tradition of a great battle having been fought on the East Mains of Dunnichen between the Picts and the Britons.
NO 51 49

City of Edinburgh

National Museum of Scotland, Chambers Street, Edinburgh: Collection of Anglian and other early medieval sculpture, including pieces from Hoddom, Aberlady, Abercorn and Morham. Also extensive collections of Dark Age material, including finds from Mote of Mark, Aberlady and Traprain Law.

Dumfries and Galloway

Ardwall Isle: an offshore island, difficult to access. Excavations in 1964–5 by Charles Thomas revealed the remains of an early chapel and burial ground. Numerous cross-slabs and cross-incised stones of eighth- to eleventh-century date, as well as

artefacts of metal, bone and glass, were recovered. Some of the finds are on display in Dumfries museum.
NX 573 495

Hoddom Old Church and graveyard: located in a ploughed field next to the River Annan, near Hoddom Bridge. The site of the church lies in the north-east corner of the graveyard, overlain by a modern burial plot and a yew tree. The excavated site formerly lay on the high river terrace to the north. It has now been removed by quarrying, and the fields reinstated, but the site gives some idea of the size and setting of the former monastery.
NY 167 727

The Ruthwell Cross

Dating to the early eighth century, the Ruthwell Cross is the most sophisticated monument of the early Northumbrian Church in Scotland. Over 5m tall, its front and back are carved with figural panels, captioned in Latin and illustrating episodes in the life of Christ and scenes associated with the early desert fathers. The sides of the shaft are filled with inhabited vine-scroll, the margins carved with Anglian runes. The runic inscription, written in Old English, contains part of the poem, 'The Dream of the Rood', spoken by the rood or cross itself on which Christ was crucified.

HISTORIC SCOTLAND

Mote of Mark: fort occupying the summit of a small rocky knoll, enclosed by a vitrified timber-laced rampart. Excavations in 1913 and 1973 produced evidence in the form of moulds, crucibles, scrap bronze and slags for extensive fine metalworking on the site. Also evidence for glass, bone and antler-working. A large assemblage of imported pottery vessels (E-ware) was also recovered. Described as a princely stronghold of late fifth to early seventh century date, the presence of two Anglian runic inscriptions and a bone comb of Anglian type suggest its later takeover by the Northumbrians. NX 845 540

Ruthwell Cross: an Anglian high cross with runic inscriptions, one of the major monuments of Dark Age Europe. There is a tradition, of uncertain age, that the cross originally stood at Priestside (NY 102 662) on the shore of the Solway. Now re-assembled inside Ruthwell parish church, it has been on the site since at least the mid-seventeenth century when it was cast down and broken by the iconoclasts after the Act 'anent the demolishing of Idolatrous Monuments'. NY 100 682

The Whithorn Trust, George Street, Whithorn: permanent exhibition and displays of artefacts from the recent excavations, and guided tours around the site of the dig, now partly laid out. An important collection of Early Christian carved stones from Whithorn and the Machars is on display in the nearby Priory Museum (HS).

East Lothian

Aberlady parish church: replica of cross-shaft, found in 1863 built into the wall of the manse garden. The broad faces are framed and divided into panels: on one face are four birds, symmetrically arranged, their necks interwoven and their legs extending into strands of interlace. On the opposite side are a pair of intertwined reptiles and below them a winged angel. The sides are decorated with a simple vine-scroll. Probably late eighth century. NT 460 798

Doon Hill, near Dunbar: the site of two successive timber halls, a polygonal palisaded enclosure and a small cemetery are marked out on the ground. The earlier hall, Hall A, is assumed to have been a British construction. Hall B, by comparison with the style of the buildings at Yeavering, is assumed to date to around the middle of the seventh century (HS). NT 687 755

Traprain Law: Iron Age hillfort and a dominant feature of the East Lothian landscape. Excavations have produced evidence for Late Bronze Age to Roman or sub-Roman occupation on the site. NT 580 747

Scottish Borders

Jedburgh Abbey: permanent exhibition in the abbey visitor centre. The displays contain a collection of Anglian sculpture from the site, including fragments of an elaborate stone shrine (HS). NT 650 204

Kirkhill, near St Abb's Head, Coldingham: the turf-covered remains of the medieval church and its burial ground are visible on the summit of the promontory. Proposed as the site of St Æbbe's monastery, founded in the 650s and described in some detail by Bede. Trenching in 1980 of the substantial rampart at the neck of the headland indicated that the turf rampart was preceded by a timber and wickerwork palisade, probably dating to the seventh or eighth century. NT 916 687

The Yarrow Stone: an Early Christian tombstone, probably of sixth-century date. It records the burials of the princes Nudus and Dumnogenus, sons of Liberalis. The stone now stands in a small enclosure beside the farm lane near the public road. NT 348 275

West Lothian

Abercorn parish church: the site of a short-lived Northumbrian bishopric in the late seventh century. An Anglo-Saxon cross-shaft, probably ninth century date, is situated inside the church. Originally standing over 4m high, the front of the shaft is divided into five roughly equal panels, 0.6m long. Set between two panels of interlace is an inhabited vine, symbolising the 'Tree of Life', represented by two birds, their wings outstretched. Above is a zoomorphic pattern, comprising two dog-like creatures, their limbs and tails intertwined. Further vine, leaf and grape-clusters are evident in the uppermost panel and along the sides of the monument. NT 081 791

Further Reading

A Gathering of Eagles: Scenes from Roman Scotland by Gordon Maxwell (Canongate 1998) examines Roman Scotland and provides the background to the emergence of the native British kingdoms in the sub-Roman period.

The Gododdin of Aneirin: text and context from Dark-Age North Britain by John T. Koch (University of Wales Press 1997). A controversial edition of the Dark Age epic poem, with a substantial historical introduction which explores the subject from a British viewpoint. Also contains a hypothetical reconstruction of the original text.

Arthur's Britain: History and Archaeology AD 367-634 by Leslie Alcock (Penguin Books 1971) is an excellent introduction to the sources and principal sites of the period.

Bede's Ecclesiastical History of the English People edited by B. Colgrave and R. A. B. Mynors (Oxford University Press 1969) is the authoritative translation and Latin text. See also *Bede: History of the English Church and People* edited by Leo Sherley-Price (Penguin Classics 1978).

The Earliest English Kings by D. P. Kirby (Routledge 1991) is a comprehensive and balanced account of the peoples and kingdoms of pre-Viking England.

Warlords and Holy Men: Scotland AD 80–1000 by Alfred P Smyth (Edward Arnold New History of Scotland, Volume 1, 1984) is an original and sometimes controversial account of Scotland in the first millennium.

The Kingdom of Northumbria AD 350–1100 by N. J. Higham (Sutton Publishing 1993) traces the history and archaeology of Northumbria, from the Roman province of Britannia Secunda to the harrying of the North

Acknowledgements

I am grateful to Olwyn Owen and Gordon Barclay for their comments on an earlier draft of this book; to Mairi Sutherland for comments and improvements to the structure of the text; to Chris Brown for his splendid reconstruction paintings and line-drawings; to Tim Holden for discussion of the plant remains from Hoddom; to Derek Hall and the staff at the Scottish Urban Archaeological Trust for the drawings of the Dunbar mortar-mixer and for permission to reproduce the pectoral cross fragment; to Alison Sheridan and the staff of the National Museum of Scotland for providing the photographs on pp. 11, 31 and 55; to Diana Murray, Kevin McLaren and the staff of the Royal Commission of the Ancient and Historical Monuments of Scotland (RCAHMS) for the illustrations on pp. 30, 32, 48 and 52; to English Heritage for the drawing on p. 35 from Tony Wilmott's Birdoswald report; to the Whithorn Trust and Suttons Publishing for permission to reproduce the drawings on pp.47 and pp. 50 respectively; and to Historic Scotland for permission to reproduce photographs. Finally, I would like to thank my family, Jane, James and Matthew, for their endurance and patience during the writing of this book.